Glimpses *of* Heaven

Glimpses
of Heaven

Gordon MacDonald
Kay Warren, Ben Patterson
Liz Curtis Higgs, Mark Buchanan
and more

HARVEST HOUSE PUBLISHERS
EUGENE, OREGON

Cover design by Left Coast Design, Portland, Oregon

Cover photo © Mettus / Shutterstock

GLIMPSES OF HEAVEN

Copyright © 2013 by Christianity Today
Published by Harvest House Publishers
Eugene, Oregon 97402
www.harvesthousepublishers.com

Library of Congress Cataloging-in-Publication Data
   Glimpses of Heaven.
      p. cm.
   ISBN 978-0-7369-5018-3 (pbk.)
   ISBN 978-0-7369-5019-0 (eBook)
   1. Christian life.
   BV4515.3.G55 2013
   242—dc23
                                                      2012026065

Printed in the United States of America

14 15 16 17 18 19 20 21 / VP-JH / 10 9 8 7 6 5 4 3

Contents

Entering the Stories of
Ordinary People   9
Gordon MacDonald

A Cheerful Giver   13
Liz Curtis Higgs

When the Bus Driver Cried   15
Ed Rowell

Thanksgiving at Fair Acres   19
Virginia Stem Owens

A Tale of Two Safari Guides   21
Mark Buchanan

Maria and the Halo   23
Barbara Royce

The Loudest Cheers in
Heaven   27
Kay Warren

Are You a Good Friend?   29
Gordon MacDonald

The Eyes of a Doctor   33
Donald Sunukjian

Up in Smoke   37
Liz Curtis Higgs

One Hot Papa   41
Ben Patterson

The Night a Robber
Dropped In   43
Connon Barclay

This Is It   47
Mark Buchanan

Treasures Old and New   51
Mark Buchanan

In God We Trust   53
Bryan Wilkerson

Diamonds Aren't Forever   55
Liz Curtis Higgs

My Conversation with God   59
Anonymous

Life Is Not like a VCR   63
Tim Brown

Garage-Sale Blues   65
Robin Lee Shope

Thy Kingdom Come   69
Mark Buchanan

White as Snow   73
Liz Curtis Higgs

New Shoes   83
Pamela Baker Powell

The Vision Thing   85
Al Hsu

The Concert of the Year   89
Mark Gauvreau Judge

A Prayer in
the Operating Room   91
Tina Blessit

Two Kinds of Thanks   93
  Evelyn Bence

A Pleasing Decision   97
  Van Morris

A Valentine's Day Dilemma   99
  Sonya Reeder

When God Interrupts   101
  Chris Erdman

A Divine Calculation   103
  Lois Spoon

The Day We Let Our
Son Live   107
  Ellen Hsu

Rewards for Honesty   111
  Bob Welch

Taskmaster   113
  Liz Curtis Higgs

No Dad to Call   117
  Heather Bermingham

A Child Is a
Bargain at Any Price   121
  Anonymous

One of Us   123
  Carol Heath

The Writing on the Wall   127
  Will Willimon

Blind to Blessing   129
  Alison Ritch

The Nightly Ritual   131
  Bob Russell

Jesus Is Missing!   133
  Greg Asimakoupoulos

The (Not So) Terrible Year   135
  Nancy Kennedy

Daddy's Baby Has Come
Home   137
  Jeannette Clift George

Living with an Intruder   139
  Dick Peterson

Flying Lesson   141
  Liz Curtis Higgs

Swords or Paintbrushes?   145
  Carla Waterman

Prayer from Far Away   147
  Peter Charpentier

The Sparrow at Starbucks   149
  John Thomas Oaks

Hiding What They Seek   153
  Carolyn Arends

A Cast of Thousands   157
  Lillian Daniel

A Purpose-Driving Life   159
  Nancy Kennedy

The 12 Days of Healing   163
  Caryl A. Harvey

An Undeliverable
Mother's Day Card   167
  Don Aycock

God Speaks Through
Unlikely People   169
  John Ortberg

Learning to Apologize   171
  Patty Kirk

Memories of Mom   175
  Bill Fix

Our Divine Distortion   177
  Carolyn Arends

Potty Break   181
  Mimi Greenwood Knight

Priceless Trust   183
  Nancy Kennedy

Tattle Tales   187
  Nancy Kennedy

Good News in
the Bad News   191
  John Ortberg

There Goes the
Neighborhood   193
  Carolyn Arends

There's a Party Going On!   197
  Max Lucado

Truer Test of Love   199
  Nancy Kennedy

Worried About Worrying   203
  Patty Kirk

What the Chicken
Told Me   207
  Gail Griner Fraga

The Christmas Tree Caper   211
  Kimberly Lynn Frost

The Holy Wanderer   215
  Richard Ryan

been waiting for you!" The woman in the wheelchair brightened and instantly retorted, "Well, let the party begin!"

He helped her with her coat, Cindy poured them coffee, and soon they were talking. I was too far away to overhear their conversation, but not so far that I couldn't appreciate the way they touched each other and maintained eye contact as they spoke. There was obvious enjoyment between them.

Stealing occasional glances in their direction, I wondered if they could have anticipated on their wedding day (55 years ago?) that a time might come when they would share a life dominated by a physical disability, a time when a simple breakfast at the Egg Shell would require special effort. Had they ever, back then, anticipated a day when the "for better or worse" clause in the marriage vows might be activated?

Watching them caused me to think back appreciatively across the years of my marriage.

When I first met Gail, love seemed such a simple, spontaneous matter. It was mostly about romance and dreams. There were valentines, chocolates, flowers, and frequent kisses. There were fantasies about homes, babies, and changing the world. Our energy and zeal for life and each other—we had little else—was in abundance. The possibility of a wheelchair never entered our minds.

A few years later, our love grew in the ups and downs of family formation: tight budgets, taking out the garbage, deciding who would comfort a child having a bad dream. We learned to communicate and cooperate, to encourage and, when necessary, to correct. We figured out that changing the world was more daunting than we'd thought. Still, we pushed ahead and found love's deeper ways.

At midlife, our love matured in the process of raising and then saying goodbye to teenagers. We had to come to grips with the physical, emotional, and spiritual changes that mark life in one's forties and fifties, and love was occasionally tested, even toughened, through disappointments and failures. Now and then we felt as if we changed a tiny bit of the world…but only a very tiny bit.

Then, not too long ago, we reached the days of Social Security checks. Now, our fiftieth anniversary looms on the horizon. But that love, once expressed by chocolates and kisses, continues to grow into something greater. It is framed in a life of grandparenting and mentoring a younger generation. It's about discovering fresh ideas and spiritual deepening. Oh, and it's about simple things like watching our diets, debating the efficacy of vitamins, and bragging about achievements in our daily workouts.

We pray more together these days. And at night—if we're not traveling—we find it easy to turn off the TV and head early for our bed, where we can hold each other closely. This love in the aging years is a deeper, more resilient kind purchased over time at great expense. Of course it's a love with scars. But underneath those scars there are no doubts.

Watching the eightysomething couple at the Egg Shell suggests still another iteration of love—one I have not experienced, but could. It's a love that comes when life's limitations—perhaps including a chronic illness or disability—accumulate and one partner must totally depend upon the other.

This version of love between two people does not just happen. It is the result of years and years of both building and discovering new layers of love's meaning so that when two people get old (really old!), they are prepared to do anything for each other and to be glad for the privilege of doing it.

The pastor in me had wanted to give something to that couple, but they beat me to the punch. Simply by being there, they unknowingly gave me a gift: a simple reminder of how beautiful aged love can be. Most young people know nothing about this.

That morning I was thankful that my friend and I had botched up our meeting time. I'd been given 30 valuable minutes to do something I'm often too busy to do. And that was to enter the stories of everyday people who like and love each other—some old guys, women friends, a mother and son, a tender husband with his beloved wife. It was a time to enjoy simple, human encounters that all too often go unnoticed.

GORDON MACDONALD

A Cheerful Giver

Christian generosity is more than just writing a check.

Christmas was approaching, the season to be generous. To give gifts to friends, donate goods to needy families, and write checks for worthy causes. Imagine my dismay when our 16-year-old son showed me I wasn't nearly as ho-ho-happy about giving as I claimed to be.

My lesson in humility began one Tuesday afternoon. Our son, Matt, sat perched on the steps of a downtown office building, waiting for his father to pick him up after his first driver training class. A man in shabby clothes ambled along, asking for money, supposedly to pay for having a tire changed at a nearby garage.

When Matt told me this story later, I felt my skin grow hot. *Yeah, right…he needed money for a tire. More like for drugs or a cheap bottle of wine.*

"The man said he needed seventeen dollars," Matt explained. "So I gave him ten."

"Ten dollars!" I fumed. How dare this panhandler talk my son out of his hard-earned money? "Honey, why would you do such a thing?"

"Because it felt good to help somebody, Mom."

Ouch. Still, I felt Matt didn't understand the situation, didn't get the Big Picture about how the world worked. "A dollar would have been plenty, Matt. Just to show him you cared."

Just to get rid of him. That's what I meant, even if I didn't say it.

Matt's brow drew into a knot. "But wouldn't ten dollars show him I cared even more?"

Ouch again. Adult logic goes by the wayside when faced with a teenager determined to do the right thing.

The Bible teaches, "If your gift is…giving, then give generously"

(Romans 12:6-8). Then why wasn't I congratulating my son for being generous instead of chastising him for being taken advantage of by a stranger on the street?

Before I could sort out my feelings, Matt confessed, "He asked me if I could spare any more, so I gave him another three dollars."

"*What!*" I threw my arms in the air, exasperated. "Son, you don't have to keep giving people money just because they ask for it! What that man did amounts to polite robbery."

"But he didn't rob me, Mom. I gave it willingly," Matt reminded me. "And it was my money. I just wanted to be kind."

Ouch, ouch, ouch.

Matt had given generously, and I called him gullible. He had given joyfully, and I robbed his joy.

He had done precisely as he'd been taught—not by me, obviously, but by the apostle Paul: "Each of you should give what you have decided in your heart to give, not reluctantly or under compulsion, for God loves a cheerful giver" (2 Corinthians 9:7).

Matt wasn't at all reluctant. But I was. He said yes to this man without feeling coerced. I would have said no and blamed the man for being pushy. My son was cheerful. I was infuriated.

Here's the saddest truth of all: I gladly write a check each December to a Christian mission for the homeless not far from the very spot where Matt did his kind deed. Sure, I'm willing to help the needy, but only if I control the amount and how it's spent. And only if I can drop my money in the mail instead of pressing it into a grimy hand.

It's embarrassing when your children teach you by example how to be more Christlike. The only thing worse is refusing to be taught. *Teach me, Lord. And forgive me when I stumble.*

If you're like my son—a cheerful giver—then may you find many opportunities to exercise your spiritual gift.

But if you're like me—a conditional giver—then may the Lord nudge your conscience, as he has mine, and show you what "cheerful giving" really means: to give without judgment. To give without hesitation. To give from the heart.

Liz Curtis Higgs

When the Bus Driver Cried

*God works through people who practice the power of
presence and who are willing to say the
things he whispers into their hearts.*

When I was in seminary, I took a job driving a school bus for kindergartners. Several of the kids came from single-parent homes. Ryan was one. As he got off the bus one day he asked me if I'd like to meet his mom sometime. "She's real pretty."

"I'll bet she is," I responded. "But I have a pretty wife at home."

Heading back to the bus barn one afternoon after finishing my route, I glanced in my mirror and saw a shaggy blond head peeping up over the last seat. "Ryan, why didn't you get off at your house?"

"I fell asleep," he said.

"When did you wake up?" I asked.

"At Kim's house," he replied.

I quizzed him further. "Well, why didn't you tell me you were still on the bus?"

Sensing my irritation, Ryan responded quietly, "I just didn't want to bother you." We circled back to his home, where he let himself in with the key hanging from a shoelace around his neck.

Halloween came. Friday afternoon, the kids were in costume, high on sugar and anticipation. Ryan was made up like a vampire. It was a long run. *Lord, just get me through this so I can go take some aspirin.* After my last stop, I scanned the bus for stowaways and headed home.

I slept in on Saturday. When I finally got moving and settled down with my first cup of coffee and the newspaper, a story on page 2 caught my eye. There had been an accident at the YMCA Halloween party.

A heavy piece of gymnastic equipment was turned over. A child was killed. It was Ryan.

I went to the White Chapel Funeral Home. My greatest fear was that I would say something that would make his parents cry. *Just don't say anything sad or stupid*, I told myself.

There were just a few people talking to Ryan's family. His mom was pretty, just as he said. His dad was there too with Ryan's stepmom. I imagined that the issues that had led to their divorce must have seemed pretty insignificant compared to the nightmare they were living right then.

I looked at the body in the half-sized casket. I thought I detected a little bit of Halloween makeup on his ear. *Don't cry, you idiot, you'll upset his parents.*

I looked up. There was no one left in the room except these three parents. I walked up to shake their hands. "I was Ryan's bus driver." His mom's eyes began to glisten. *Watch it, don't get her started.*

I told them about the day Ryan fell asleep on the bus and missed his stop. Even as they laughed at his response—"I didn't want to bother you"—I could see the tears begin to well up in everyone's eyes. *Way to go, Ed. Now you've made them all cry.*

Ryan's mom started to speak and then grabbed me tight and started shaking with those choking sobs that I dreaded worse than anything. To make matters worse, I started crying too. Not discreetly, but all noisy and messy. I held this young mother I'd never met before and wished I had something to say that would turn their attention away from my tears and runny nose.

A thought came to me. It sounded good until I said it aloud. "Just remember," I said when we all quieted down a little, "God knows the pain of losing a son too." With those words, another wave of grief crashed over us.

As soon as I could, I got out of there. I feared I had poured salt in the wounded hearts of those parents.

The months passed quickly. Christmas came and went. My midterm exams were on the horizon. One Saturday, I spent the whole day studying and nursing a stomachache that wouldn't go away. Finally, I called my doctor. "You'd better get to the emergency room. Sounds like appendicitis to me." My wife drove me over right away.

As I lay there on the gurney, waiting for tests before surgery, a shot of something warm took the edge off the pain. In walked a pretty, young woman in white. She looked like Ryan's mom. *You're hallucinating*, I told myself.

"Hello, bus driver," she said with a smile. It was her—with a needle in her hand.

"I want to thank you for being there that night," she said as she tightened the tourniquet until my veins popped out. "I can't tell you how much your words about God understanding have helped me over these past few months." She slipped the needle in—I never even felt it. "But the fact that you cared enough to cry with us meant more than anything."

ED ROWELL

Thanksgiving at Fair Acres

The holiday takes on new meaning at a nursing home.

The tables have been rearranged end-to-end, pilgrim-style, for the Thanksgiving feast, and my father and I take our places on either side of my mother. Across from us sit Norman, the owner of the Christian music boom box, and James, a black man in a Mister Rogers cardigan who moves with glacial stateliness to compensate for his halting, stroke-damaged gait. They maintain their usual distant reserve.

"May we join you?" I ask, making my voice bright with what I hope they will see as holiday cheer. James inclines his head in a courtly manner. Norman says, "Sure," and blinks several times in what appears to be welcome.

"Isn't this nice," I say enthusiastically, gesturing toward the centerpieces—baskets of orange, yellow, and red silk leaves, accented with stalks of dried grass and little plastic ears of corn. James nods; Norman says, "Yes, nice." My father grins.

Meanwhile, an aide is maneuvering the wheelchair of a woman with a rust-colored perm and a silk blouse into position across from my father. Her head shakes like Katharine Hepburn's, and in one hand she clutches a washcloth with which she continually dabs at her mouth. The washcloth, I see, is to mop up saliva pushed toward the front of her mouth by her tongue, which squirms compulsively like a small burrowing animal.

Over the kitchen clatter, I shout inanities across the table at Norman and James alternately. "Smell that? Mmm, turkey!" "What kind of pie are you going to have, pumpkin or pecan?" "Want a roll to tide you over?"

Amid great bustle, the food is brought from the kitchen and laid out buffet-style. I load a plate with turkey, dressing, gravy, sweet potatoes, fruit salad, cranberry sauce—the dishes I know my mother has always liked. After cutting the turkey into bite-sized bits, I name the plate's contents, coaxing her appetite. "Take a bite of the dressing, Mother, you'll like it." She ignores me, making her way slowly but steadily through the turkey.

"Would you like another roll? I'll butter it for you."

She shakes her head and, after finishing the turkey, puts down her fork, leaving the rest of the meal untouched. The noise, I know, distracts her. The sounds are a jumble she can't sort into meaning.

Telling my father to finish at his own pace, I wheel my mother back to her room. We're both relieved by the quiet that settles around us there. I press the call button for the aides to come and lift her into bed, and then I sit beside her, holding her hand until she drops into a fitful sleep.

"How did the nursing home dinner go?" my daughter asked me the following week as we were recovering from the "real" Thanksgiving feast.

"You know that parable in Luke where the master sends his servant out to the highways and hedges to bring in the maimed, the halt, and the blind after the people he'd invited to the banquet don't show up?"

"Mmm…I think so."

"Well, that's how it was. And I got to come too."

VIRGINIA STEM OWENS

A Tale of Two Safari Guides

*Our ability to see is determined in part by
our willingness to pay attention.*

Twice I've visited heaven, or close to it: the Masai Mara, perhaps the greatest wildlife preserve in the world. The Masai Mara is part of the vast grasslands that stretch over the fertile plains of East Africa. Here, elephant, cheetah, gazelle, wildebeest, water buffalo, giraffe, crocodile, rhinoceros, hippopotamus, and hundreds of other furry or scaly, tusked or horned, fleet-foot or slithering, flying or crawling, night-stalking or sun-loving creatures roam and soar and wade and burrow without fear of man.

But the guides I had for the two trips could not have been more different from one another. The first guide, Stephen, made the trip a thing of joy and wonder and endless surprise. The second guide, William, almost ruined the trip entirely.

The difference was one thing: Stephen paid attention and William didn't. Stephen had good eyes and William didn't. I'm not referring to the power and clarity of their organ of sight. No, Stephen looked at the right thing at the right time with the right focus, and William didn't.

Stephen was a Masai man in his early twenties who grew up a few miles from the very ground we crossed together. The land was in his blood—every hillock and grove and bend of river. He knew in his bones the personal histories of many of the animals we saw. He had an intuition for finding animals that seemed supernatural, at least to a white suburban guy like me who thinks that spotting a squirrel is a major wildlife event. He would stop and gaze at something two kilometers in the distance. It looked to me like more grass and acacia, but he would drive toward it. Maybe 300 yards away, I'd finally see what he saw: a mother rhino and its baby grazing in scrub brush or a pride of lions sleeping beneath a tree or a pair of cheetahs sunning themselves on a shelf of rock.

William was a Comba man in his midfifties who grew up in Nairobi. He couldn't see for looking—but he wasn't looking anyhow. He spent most of his time chatting on his CB with his friends. He just followed the crowd. Wherever other vehicles congested, he went. We saw the animals, yes. But we saw them from within a swarm of dozens—sometimes hundreds—of other sightseers, each jockeying for a better view. One time we were traveling alone from the pack. A herd of elephants grazed at the roadside, mere feet away. William sailed past them because he didn't see them.

"William!" we yelled. "Elephants!"

"Huh? Where?"

I tell you about Stephen and William to tell you this: The kingdom of God is at hand. Pay attention. You could miss it entirely if you choose to look at the wrong thing.

MARK BUCHANAN

Maria and the Halo

Sometimes things happen that doctors can't explain.

Every other Tuesday, Maria Lopez came to clean my house.

Maria always arrived like a bubble of energy determined to restore order to my universe, scrubbing as though it were an act of worship.

As we became acquainted, I learned that Maria was a pastor's daughter from Peru who had no family in the United States. I had been a Christian for only a few years and appreciated Maria's enthusiastic faith. She prayed out loud while she vacuumed and sang praise songs in Spanish while she scrubbed. She praised Jesus everywhere she went.

One Tuesday, Maria didn't show up for work. I anticipated seeing her cheery face the following day, but no one came.

When she didn't arrive the next day, I called. No one answered the phone.

This is so unlike her, I thought. *She's so reliable. There must be a good reason.*

On the third day, a nurse called to say Maria was at the hospital. Alarmed, I cut some flowers and drove to Northridge Hospital to find out what was wrong. I found Maria sitting up in bed, rocking back and forth with her head encased in a heavy iron cage resting on her shoulders. Her eyes were closed, and tears streamed down her cheeks. Touching her arm gently, I held out the flowers. She clutched them to her chest.

"What's that around your head, Maria?"

"Oooh, Meessus," she moaned, touching the iron contraption, "it is the torture of Satan."

Puzzled, I turned to the nurse. She explained, "It's called a halo. It's screwed and bolted directly into the skull in four different places. It isn't pleasant."

"How long must you wear it?" I asked Maria.

"Five months, my doctor say, maybe. But Meessus, you tell him, Maria, she no live five months with thees in her head. She die. You tell him, yes?"

"I'll talk to him, Maria. Anything else I can do for you?"

"Yes, Meessus. My Bible." She pointed to the bedside table. "Please, you read to me."

"Sure, Maria."

I started reading John 14. "Do not let your hearts be troubled. You believe in God; believe also in me."

Out in the corridor, I found Maria's doctor. "Why is she wearing that hideous device?"

"Because, to put it simply, if she didn't," he said, "her head would fall off. Maria has cancer. Her neck bones have degenerated to the point where they can no longer support her head."

"Can they be repaired? Or regenerated?"

He shook his head gravely. "It means we can't ever take it off. Maria will have to get used to living with it."

Every week when I visited, Maria asked me to pray with her and read from the Bible. She always requested the same chapter from the New Testament: John 14. Weeks turned into months. The heavy metal halo was crippling.

During one visit, months after being admitted to the hospital, Maria clutched my hands and whispered, "God tells Maria it won't be long. Soon, he say, we take this off."

Before I left the hospital, I stopped at the nurses' desk to ask how much longer Maria would be there. A nurse said they were preparing papers to release her. *Maria doesn't have insurance or enough money to stay in the hospital. That's why they're releasing her.*

Maria panicked when the doctor told her she must leave. "No! You take new X-ray." Touching the halo she cried, "You take this torture from me! I no leave with this!"

"There is really no point," he insisted. "Nothing has changed."

When I returned to the hospital two days later to pick up Maria, I was surprised to find her sitting in a chair, beaming ear to ear. "I no leave today," she said.

"Why not, Maria? Have you had your X-ray?"

"Yes. But I stay until they take this off." She rolled her eyes toward the halo.

Hasn't anyone told Maria what will happen when they take the halo off? It was my turn to panic. *I can't tell her. Her despair will be overwhelming.*

I cornered the doctor. "She won't leave until you take the halo off. What do we do?"

"We'll take it off," he replied.

"You said her head will roll off without it!"

Maria's doctor began acting strangely. He looked left and right and then muttered, "It won't roll. The X-ray we took this morning indicated her neck bones have regenerated."

"You said that was impossible."

"It is impossible."

I shook my head, confused. "Were the original X-rays a mistake?"

"Not at all. They're here for anyone to see."

"So?"

Before answering, the doctor sighed. "So there are things I can't explain. Her bones have regenerated, and they are strong enough to hold her head. That's all I know."

"Doctor! Is this a miracle?"

"I don't know about miracles—that's Maria's department. She tells me Jesus healed her."

BARBARA ROYCE

The Loudest Cheers in Heaven

*Celebrating the return of our troops reminds
us of the power of encouragement.*

Heading home to California, a friend and I passed through the Dallas–Fort Worth airport. On the way to the connecting gate, we heard loud patriotic music playing and saw a group, mostly women, wearing colorful hats, cheering, and waving American flags. The troops were coming home, and here was their welcoming committee.

Two women encouraged us to grab flags and join in. We were early for our next flight, so we took places in the makeshift greeting line. At first, just a few soldiers dribbled by. We whooped and waved our flags furiously. Then the pace picked up as dozens of men and women in uniform came barreling through. We kept repeating, "Welcome home! We're glad you're back! We appreciate you!" Some soldiers wiped away tears while others displayed huge, self-conscious smiles.

After 45 minutes, it was time to catch our flight. We hugged the organizers and thanked the older vets who had come to honor this generation of soldiers. As we sank into our seats for the flight, we felt humbled by participating in this sweet moment of coming home. It was impossible not to draw the obvious spiritual parallels. These men and women had taken oaths of faithfulness and service. They fought courageously, took unbelievable risks, and lived with deprivation, danger, and disease, all for the good of our nation.

But as great as America is, it is a temporary place. No nation lives forever. As believers in Christ, we are all soldiers in the Lord's army. We, too, take oaths of fidelity, sacrifice, and service. Our oaths of allegiance are to a kingdom that will never end—a country where there is never a mistake in leadership, where justice flows down like a river, where poverty, disease, terror, hunger, and greed hold no power.

Scripture teaches us about the welcome and rewards we will receive when our battle on earth is over. Artists, writers, and theologians have all taken stabs at imagining what those moments of heavenly welcome will look like. That afternoon, we were visualizing the very moment when we would step into eternity.

As my friend Elizabeth and I looked at each other, the same thought crossed our minds. Through misty eyes, she said, "If I get there first, I'll be on your welcoming committee. I'll be jumping up and down, screaming, 'You made it! I'm so proud of you!'"

I laughed and said, "Oh, you're not going to beat me. I'm older. I'll be at the head of the line to greet you!" In that moment, heaven was more real than the smell of the stale coffee in our foam cups.

What I'm really wondering about is this: Will we be surprised at who gets the biggest welcome? I'm not coveting more high-fives, but I am dimly aware of something so profound and holy that I can barely put it into words.

All of us fight unseen battles every day, each believer a secret soldier locked in battle with forces no one else can see. The bravest among us are not necessarily those who fight with guns or tanks. The bravest person you know might be your husband or wife or neighbor or coworker who goes on living one more day when every bone in his or her body says it's no use.

How much could we lighten the load for another just by telling him how brave we think he is? Oh, to be so merciful with fellow soldiers fighting their personal, hidden wars.

Best of all, how much better when we bring undisclosed struggles into community, where victories can be celebrated together, great losses can be mourned together, and whoops of encouragement can provide even the weariest soldier the courage to keep on keeping on for one more day.

KAY WARREN

Are You a Good Friend?

*A dangerous mountain hike provides a
lesson about true friendship.*

I once traveled with three close men-friends to Switzerland and spent eight days walking the *Wanderweg* trail system in the Alps. One of those walks was high above the town of Grindelwald. It was a beautiful day, and our spirits soared in response to the alpine grandeur. And so did our self-confidence. Rather than take a pathway of realistic length and difficulty for three men in their sixties and one in his seventies, we chose one requiring much greater exertion. Not smart.

Three miles into the walk, my friend Al (the man in his seventies) became exhausted, seriously so. Turning back was not an option. I proposed to the other men that they walk on ahead to the end of the trail and secure rooms for us in a *berghaus* (mountain hotel) because it would be impossible for us to return to our regular lodgings for the night. Al and I then sat down to plot our strategy.

I suggested that we take 100 steps and rest for three minutes, another 100 steps and rest for three minutes. If we were going uphill, he would lead; if downhill, I would lead. This simple routine, I thought, would give order to our situation. Al agreed, and we started walking again, now very, very slowly. We had three miles to walk in 100-step increments, and it took almost five hours.

Al and I walked arm in arm as two lovers might walk in the park. Most men are normally self-conscious about any kind of touching. But that day this was not an issue. I constantly spoke words of encouragement into the ear of my friend. I quoted Scripture, told stories, recalled sermons, intermittently prayed, and frequently reminded him of experiences we'd shared over the years of our friendship. I thought of every word that described my friend, and I commented on each of them for him. Words like brave, quiet-spirited or humble, sacrificial, faithful, gentle, generous. Finally, just as darkness fell, we reached the *berghaus* the other men had found for us.

Since that time, Al and I (and the others) have spoken of that unforgettable afternoon when two old guys struggled to reach the end of the trail. We have often recalled the spoken words of encouragement, the shared strength, even the affection that came with the encouragement. I have never felt closer to another male friend than I did that afternoon. Often Al and I have said to each other, "If I live to be a hundred, I'll never forget that day."

This past month, I lost my friend Al to cancer, and I cannot describe the hurt of the loss. His wife, Lena, our other friends, my wife, Gail, and I (along with hundreds of others) stood at the edge of his open grave and grieved. At Al's funeral I told the story of our day in the Alps and the way we talked each other through a threatening experience. And I spoke of genuine friendship—the sweetness of Christian brothers (or sisters) generating mutual courage on the journey. Why, I asked, are we tricked into thinking that achievement and accumulation are the secret of success when, in fact, real success begins with the building of a few personal relationships which become so precious that you would die—without hesitation—for your friends?

I fear for too many in Christian work whose relationships (even marriages) are defined by some institutional function, relationships that will weaken and dissolve soon after the function does. Such people may recognize one day they have no one to die with, and dying alone is not a good idea.

Recently, while on a long flight, I read Nelson Mandela's autobiography. What got him through 27 years of imprisonment? This was his answer.

> The authorities' greatest mistake was to keep us [leaders in the anti-apartheid movement who'd been arrested] together, for together our determination was reinforced.

We supported each other and gained strength from each other. Whatever we knew, whatever we learned, we shared, and by sharing we multiplied whatever courage we had individually. That is not to say that we were all alike in our responses to the hardships we suffered. Men have different capacities and react differently to stress. But the stronger ones raised up the weaker ones, and both became stronger in the process.

Sounds like 100 steps and rest, 100 steps and rest.

GORDON MACDONALD

The Eyes of a Doctor

The role we play—judge or doctor—determines what we see.

Let's suppose that on your way to work in the morning, you usually stop at a Starbucks. You tend to get to the store at the same time, and you usually see a young girl who gets there about the same time you do. On many mornings you find yourselves standing next to each other in line. In fact, you both order the same thing—double espresso with skim milk.

She seems to be into the Goth culture—black hair, black clothes, knee-high jackboots, black fingernails, black lipstick, scattered tattoos, and piercings in the nose, lips, ears, and eyebrows. She usually has a backpack that she has to take off to get her money, and sometimes she seems to struggle to hold the backpack, get the money, and pay for the coffee all at the same time.

She doesn't make too much eye contact with others. You wonder whether you should strike up a conversation with her—maybe offer to hold her backpack while she pays. You're not sure what to do with the whole Goth bit, and you don't know whether she'd give you a dark look and not say anything.

Should you try to be friendly? Maybe find out what brings you both to the same Starbucks each morning? See if she ever tries any of the other specialty coffees? Move toward greeting her each morning? Learn about other parts of her life?

Yes! By all means! Move into her world. Make a comment one day about how the barista probably already knows both of your orders as soon as you walk in the door. Offer to hold her backpack while she pays. A couple of days later, tell her your name and ask for hers. If she misses a few days, tell her you hope she wasn't sick the next time you see her.

Why move into her world? Because with the eyes of a doctor, you see her pain. You see anger and alienation. Maybe it's because of sexual abuse from a stepfather, a brother, or an old boyfriend. But you see the heaviness, the sadness. With the eyes of a doctor, you see a hurt that God can heal.

There's a man at work that everybody shakes their head at. He's been divorced a couple of times, and both of his ex-wives are suing him for past child support. He's a deadbeat dad—way behind on his support, sending them just a little bit every so often. He's been living with another woman and her small child, but a couple of weeks ago, he slapped her around pretty hard. She called the cops, he spent a couple nights in jail, and she kicked him out and now has a restraining order against him. He's currently living in a cheap motel that rents by the month.

Every day at lunch, he goes out by himself to get a hamburger or a burrito, always coming back with mustard or chili on his shirt. Nobody says much to him because he's too quick to complain about how everybody's taking advantage of him, everybody's pushing his buttons, everybody's squeezing him dry. Who wants to listen to that?

You've often wondered about being nice and offering to go to lunch with him. You like the same fast food he does—Burger King and Taco Bell and Subway. And you know Subway has a sale going on—three foot-long sandwiches for ten dollars. You couldn't possibly eat that much, but it seems like a shame not to take advantage of such a bargain. Should you invite him along one day?

Yes! By all means! Move into his world. Go to lunch with him. When you get to Subway and you both sit down with your sandwiches and chips and drinks, ask him if he's watched any of the baseball playoffs. Who's he rooting for in the World Series? Mention that it's been just about the worst umpiring you've ever seen.

Why move into his world? Because with the eyes of a doctor, you see his pain. You see bitterness in life, failure at relationships, blaming others instead of knowing how to change himself. You sense his fear of the future—no money and now a criminal record—and his desperation about being all alone in the world. With the eyes of a doctor, you see a hurt that God can heal.

Your company has a coed softball team that competes in the city league, and they're looking for a couple of extra players. You like softball. You like the feel of connecting on a pitch, running down a fly ball, making a clothesline throw on one hop to home plate to nail a runner trying to score. The first game is next Tuesday, and they're pushing you to join them.

But you're not sure. You like softball, but you don't know about playing with the people in the office. You went to a company picnic a couple of months ago, and some of the guys at the pickup softball game were drinking a lot of beer and making some pretty raunchy comments about some of the women on the other team. Some of the wives of your coworkers were loudmouthed, and they flirted with other husbands. The parents yelled mean things at their children but did nothing to control them. And in the parking lot, one of the married men from the office who had come to the picnic by himself was behind his pickup truck going at it pretty heavy with one of the single moms in the office. Do you want to deal with all that every week? Should you join the team?

Yes! By all means! Move into their world. Get to the park, shag those balls, and run those bases. Bring some Cokes to put in with their beers. When one of the women on the other team lines it into a gap between center and left for a stand-up double, instead of questioning her sexual preference, shout out, "Great hit! Did you play in college?" Buy a cheap glove for the single mom's kid, ask if he wants to be batboy, have him sit beside you on the bench, and teach him the strategies of the game.

Why move into their world? Because with the eyes of a doctor, you see their pain. You see that the machismo and the raunchiness merely disguise insecurity and failure. You see marriages without love and children without the security of boundaries. You see the single mom's loneliness and vulnerability that puts her at risk of being deeply hurt. With the eyes of a doctor, you see the hurts that God can heal.

In life we can have the eyes of a judge or we can have the eyes of a doctor. With the eyes of a judge, we see a Goth girl, a deadbeat dad, and a foulmouthed team, and we think, *Why have anything to do with them?* With the eyes of a doctor, we see the hurts that God can heal.

DONALD SUNUKJIAN

Up in Smoke

I'd followed God's lead, and this was the result?

"God moves in a mysterious way." This doesn't appear in the Bible—British poet William Cowper wrote those words in 1774—but *mysterious* well describes an experience that took me years to understand.

When our children were younger, we employed a hardworking woman to clean our house each week. An enthusiastic Christian, she lived from paycheck to paycheck, always struggling financially yet never losing her joy in the Lord.

One spring Tuesday, instead of driving up in her rusty Toyota, she climbed out of a friend's car and dragged her cleaning supplies through the kitchen door, trying hard not to look dejected. "My old car finally quit for good," she explained. "I found another one just like it at a used car lot, but I don't have twelve dollars to spare, let alone twelve hundred."

I commiserated with her and promised I'd pray for God's provision.

But my conscience wouldn't let the subject rest. *She needs a car, Liz. God has blessed you...can't you bless her?* Verses from past sermons prodded me: "The righteous give without sparing" (Proverbs 21:26) and "Be generous and willing to share" (1 Timothy 6:18).

The Lord made it abundantly clear what he expected of me. But what about my frugal (okay, *tight*) husband, Bill? Would he get the same message?

Bill not only said yes but also escorted her to the dealership and dutifully kicked the tires. Such a good man.

The following Tuesday she drove up to our house, tooting her horn and grinning from ear to ear. "Even if it takes me years to pay you back, it's worth it," she insisted. "How can I ever thank you?"

I smiled back at her. "By letting us simply give it to you." I didn't want our working relationship to hinge on an unpaid loan. How much better to make it a gift rather than a business transaction.

If my story ended on this happy note, you might think what fine, generous Christians we are. But that won't do. The car was the Lord's idea, not ours, and it was paid for with his money. Bill and I were little more than conduits.

Besides, the story isn't over.

The next Saturday at midnight, our phone rang. I leaped from the bed and grabbed the receiver, my heart in my throat. Was a family member ill? Injured? Dying?

"Oh, Liz..." It was the strained voice of our house cleaner. "It's...my car...it's *gone*."

I listened in disbelief as she told her sad tale. An unstable neighbor in her apartment building had set her Toyota on fire. Burned it to ashes for no reason at all.

"He *torched* your car?" Whoever heard of such a thing? After exhaling with frustration, I offered what comfort I could. "At least your insurance will cover it."

"But I don't...have...insurance."

I gripped the phone, furious with the nameless pyro and angry with myself for not making certain she was insured.

"Please, Liz...please don't be mad. I can pay you back."

"Don't be silly," I chided her gently, releasing the last traces of my anger into the darkened room. "The fire wasn't your fault, sweetie. And anyway, your car was a gift."

Some gift, Lord. What happened? Weren't we generous enough? Wasn't she needy enough?

Even after her son managed to get her old car working, I struggled over the strange turn of events. Had we missed something? Some lesson we were supposed to learn, some undiscovered truth?

Jesus once said to his disciples, "You do not realize now what I am doing, but later you will understand" (John 13:7).

A decade later, what I understand is this: God calls us to be obedient and to trust in him. Even when we can't see why or how things work out the way they do. Even when the results don't seem to make sense.

Though God's way may be mysterious, his love is fully insured. And his grace is blessedly fireproof.

LIZ CURTIS HIGGS

One Hot Papa

*We look our best when we don't
pretend to be something we're not.*

Blythe is a desert town on the Arizona–California border. My family and I were on our way back home from vacation when we stopped at a McDonald's in Blythe. Lauretta, my wife, asked me to hold Mary, our eighteen-month-old, while she went to the restroom and our three sons romped in the play area.

Picture me holding my daughter, a few feet from the restroom doors, as "The Babe from Blythe" emerged from behind those doors. She was gorgeous—tanned and dressed as, well, as young women are wont to dress in warm desert climates.

And she was smiling right at me! I straightened up and smiled back, flush with the adolescent conceit that even though I was much older than she was, I must still be a very attractive man. Babes still take notice!

Our smiles and eyes met for longer than a mere random encounter as she walked past. Then I noticed my reflection in the mirror along the wall and saw the person she was smiling at. It was me, all right, but it wasn't Ben Patterson the Mature Hunk. It was Ben Patterson, Mary's Daddy. He was middle-aged, a little lumpy, and holding a precious child. That's what delighted the Babe.

My first reaction was embarrassment. *Silly fool, you aren't what you thought you were!*

But as I continued to look in the mirror, I decided I liked what I saw there more than I liked what I first thought the Babe saw. I like being Mary's daddy. I like it a lot. Ditto for Dan and Joel and Andy. It's better to be a daddy than a stud. My deflation turned into elation.

BEN PATTERSON

The Night a Robber Dropped In

A botched burglary led to an unforgettable Christmas.

As a young college student I did not have much money. For me, hitting the books was easy, but putting my feet to the pavement was a chore.

Family members wondered about my sanity when I rented one of two small apartments on the second floor of a burned-out furniture store. The building had been condemned, but the price for living in such an ugly place was budget-beautiful. After years of middle-class comfort, I was also spending the year without a car. My only real possessions were a used black-and-white portable television, a typewriter, and a card table that I used for a desk.

Though my living quarters were tiny, they were quiet and certainly secure. Who would walk on the roof next to my windows? The holes in the roof were still not repaired from the fire.

One night I left my television on, posing as a night-light. I'd fallen asleep on what years before had been a couch. A book with too many 50-cent words lulled me into dreamland. About five feet from my head was one of two windows I had fashionably covered with scissored sheets.

The Christmas season was in full stride. However, my apartment lacked the wonderful smell of a freshly decorated tree; instead, I'd been trying to air out the place from an unfortunate kitchen incident with a burned meat loaf. My window was open several inches more than usual.

It was way past midnight when I heard the window go up quickly and suddenly. A sneaker-clad foot stepped through the opening.

What do you do when someone enters your window uninvited? This hadn't been covered in my home economics class. My feet still ached from carrying the TV from a garage sale 100 blocks away, and I needed my typewriter and card table, so I wasn't about to be generous. I lunged for the leg and arm.

I missed. The would-be intruder twisted, jumped out the window, and ran across the roof. With only sock traction, I headed him off at street level, meeting him just as he jumped from the low roof.

My adrenaline was pumping, and I almost killed the kid as I apprehended him. He started to cry as I forced him upstairs so I could call the police.

My neighborhood had more than its share of patrol cars, and three arrived within minutes. The police handcuffed the teenager and took him down to a police cruiser. I followed along.

Then it was back to my apartment with two officers to show them the window the robber thought was a door. The third officer stayed in the cruiser, filling out a report.

The officers explained the procedure—the teenager would be taken to jail, and I needed to contact the prosecutor's office.

Just then, the two officers started arguing. "We need to rid our streets of drug addicts like the bum you caught," the first officer started. "You told us, Mr. Barclay, you could not understand why anyone would rob you. Obviously, he saw the light from your TV and thought it was something he could trade for drugs."

The other officer put me on the spot. Despite his partner's objections, he explained the 17-year-old offender's background—he already had a police record. The teen came from an abusive family situation and had been expelled from school. His entire family disowned him, and he was on probation for previous robberies.

"If you press charges, he'll go to prison," the officer concluded. "But if you'll agree not to press charges, I'll promise to get him into a counseling center for addicts so he and his family can be rehabilitated."

Could I deny this young person one more chance if someone believed in him so much?

The first officer noticed my hesitation. "If you go easy on him, his friends will hear and they'll be coming in your window next!" He also reminded me that if the boy had been armed, I could have been seriously injured.

He was right. But still, the other officer's willingness to go against his partner and personally follow up on the young robber was impressive. *I've needed some second chances over the years,* I thought as past kindnesses came to mind. I couldn't deny giving the boy's future over to the caring officer.

The next few days and all through Christmas, I felt good knowing I had given something worth more than a few nicely wrapped presents.

Frankly, I did nail down the window until I could find my next address…one that didn't have an easy roof access. In the subsequent months, I looked for the boy's name in the paper but never saw it, nor did I hear anything more.

The following Christmas I received a card from the kind police officer. "Wanted to let you know counseling seemed to work and the boy has been reunited with some caring members of his family. He should do well. I trust only Santa is coming through your windows at your new address. Have a Merry Christmas!"

I did indeed.

CONNON BARCLAY

This Is It

*We may struggle to define community, but
we know when we experience it.*

A few years ago, a friend assembled a weekend work party to lay sod in his yard. The sun was shining. He had fresh coffee and cinnamon buns. And the workers he'd called together were all good friends. We liked each other immensely.

Then Al said, "Guys, do you realize something? This is it! This is it!" We stopped.

"Al, this is what?"

"This is community."

We all murmured our assent and congratulated one another. Yes. This is it.

But then I said, "Al, this is great, but I don't think this is it. I like you all too much. Add a person or two to this company who lacks social graces, who looks different, who's needy, smelly, and irritating. If we truly loved a person like that, then that would be it."

Silence. Then one of the guys said, "Uh, Mark...we've accepted you, haven't we?"

We all laughed, but they granted my point.

We're always tempted to turn the church into a club. With our kind of people. With a strict decorum designed to keep up appearances and keep out the...shall we say, undesirables. But Jesus said it's no credit to us if we love those who love us—our kind of people. We don't need God to love them; natural affinities are sufficient. But we, Jesus said, are to love the least and the worst—the losers, the enemies. That takes

God: a supernatural subversion of our own prejudices and a heaven-borne infusion of God's prodigal love.

I preach that. I try to live that.

A year or so after our sod-laying party, Wanda arrived. Wanda was not our kind of people. She was thirsty all right—for beer, port, rum, vanilla extract, whatever. She had only one way to pay for that. I'll let you guess.

But she was desperately thirsty for something else too. She called the church one day, wondering if she could see a pastor—right now. Two of us met with her. She told us her troubled story. I told her about the woman at the well whose life, like Wanda's, wasn't going well. But she met Jesus, and he offered her living water. I explained what living water was and asked Wanda if she'd like some.

"Oh yeah!" she said. We prayed. She confessed, repented, surrendered. Drank deep.

The other pastor said, "Now, Wanda, this Sunday will be your first time in church. Don't feel you have to fit in right away. You can sit at the back if you like, come late, leave early. Whatever is comfortable."

Wanda looked at him sideways. "Why would I do that?" she said. "I've been waiting for this all my life."

That Sunday, Wanda was the first to arrive. She sat at the front and loudly agreed with everything I said. She was the last to leave. Same thing the next Sunday, except she brought a friend, one of her kind of people. I preached on servanthood. My main point: If you've tasted the love of Jesus, you'll want to serve. It was Communion Sunday. In those days, we called our elders the Servant Leadership Team. I asked the Servant Leaders to come and help with Communion. That day only two of our team were in church. They straggled to the front.

All Wanda heard was the word *servant*. And she had been listening intently to my sermon: If you've tasted the love of Jesus, you'll want to serve.

She walked straight up to serve Communion with the other two "servants."

I flinched.

Then I remembered Luke 7, Jesus's words to Simon the Pharisee as a woman, not unlike Wanda, washed Jesus's feet: "Do you see this woman?"

Do you see her?

I leaned over to Wanda and said, "Since this is your very first time doing this, do you mind if I help?"

So Wanda and I served Communion. The best part was watching the faces of the people I love and serve and pray for and preach to.

Not one flinched. They saw her.

This is it.

MARK BUCHANAN

Treasures Old and New

*Mark Buchanan continues the compelling
story about a woman named Wanda.*

Wanda did well for about eight months—got into Alpha and a 12-step group and got her kids back. Then she didn't do well, in and out of rehab—mostly out. Then she vanished. Then one day she called again, sober, after a year in rehab in Vancouver. She was getting out the next week. Could she come home? Her first Sunday back, I initially didn't recognize her. She looked healthy. Dressed and in her right mind.

I was preaching on the ten lepers Jesus healed, and the one, a Samaritan, who returned to give thanks. I said that those who have been cleansed by Jesus, who want to be made whole by him, worship at his feet in deep thankfulness, in utmost desperation. They have nowhere else they want to go. And then, to close, I reminded people we have a tradition at our church: Anyone can come up to the front and pray with one of our prayer ministers. Wanda came forward. But she didn't go to a prayer minister. She walked onto the platform, between the guitarist and the drummer, and stretched her hands heavenward. She worshipped like one leper returning. A woman who didn't know her, and who isn't on the prayer team, walked up, put her arm around her, and worshipped too. Then—you could hear it—all of us worshipped with deeper thankfulness, out of greater desperation. Out of the storeroom had come new treasures as well as old, and the kingdom hovered very close.

MARK BUCHANAN

In God We Trust

God gives what's best to those who leave the choice to him.

Charlie and Agnes are two of the meekest people I've ever known. Charlie is a bright, energetic, hardworking man who could have been successful at just about anything he set out to do. What he set out to do was mission work. He spent his entire career working with some of the lowliest people on earth—alcoholics on skid row. For many years he was director of Pacific Garden Mission in Chicago, and then in his retirement years he went to work for the McCauley Water Street Mission in New York. At a time in life when most people his age were playing golf or taking cruises, Charlie would commute every day to minister to homeless men on the streets of New York.

You don't get rich doing mission work your whole life, but every once in a while, Charlie and his wife, Agnes, would get to do something special. One year they invited my wife, Karen, and me to join them for a night on the town. Someone had given them tickets to hear Handel's *Messiah* at Carnegie Hall—velvet-covered seats in a private booth. It was a great night, and we all enjoyed it.

As they drove us home that night, Karen and I were sitting in the backseat, and I was admiring Charlie and Agnes. They were all dressed up for their big night out. She was sitting close to him as if they were high school sweethearts. They struck me in that moment as two of the happiest people on earth. Just then I noticed a little plaque they had stuck to the dashboard of their old Chevy. It explained everything: "God gives what's best to those who leave the choice to him."

Charlie and Agnes had long ago given up striving, fretting, and demanding things from God and from life. Instead they had surrendered to God their talents, their careers, their safety, their material needs, and even their retirement. Instead of chasing the abundant life, they waited for God to bring it to them.

BRYAN WILKERSON

Diamonds Aren't Forever

While shopping for my engagement ring, I learned what's really valuable.

Each March when our anniversary rolls around, Bill and I curl up on the couch and watch the videotape of our wedding ceremony, shaking our heads at the two vaguely familiar young people grinning their way down the aisle. I'm just grateful a camera crew wasn't around to capture every moment during our four-month engagement.

Like the night Bill and I went shopping for my engagement ring soon after he popped the question. No way do I want to see that on instant replay.

The jeweler watched as we touched the loose diamonds she'd strewn across a square of blue velvet. "What's your budget?" she asked, her tone hopeful.

Bill gulped. "Four hundred." On a college teacher's salary it was all he could afford, but I still winced. Four hundred dollars meant a very small diamond. Teeny tiny. Except for the flaws. Those would be huge.

The jeweler merely smiled and guided us to the other end of the counter. "I think we can find something here that will suit you." Out came another velvet square, but the diamond chips she placed on it nearly disappeared in the nap of the fabric.

As Bill listened to the jeweler explain carat weight, my gaze drifted back to the larger stones. Their facets caught the bright store lights, beckoning me.

Diamonds are forever. Store-bought eternity looked good that wintry evening.

We finally chose a pretty but petite gemstone. Only a jeweler would notice the flaw. As small as it was, the diamond still twinkled nicely.

Bill touched my elbow. "Make sure you're happy with it, Liz, while I look around."

Happy? I was happy with him, no doubts there. Settling for a diminutive diamond was another story. As a single woman I'd grown accustomed to buying whatever I wanted and worrying about how things got paid for later. My frugal fiancé, though, was a cash-and-carry kind of guy.

But he did say he wanted me to be happy…

Once he was out of earshot, I waved the woman closer. "May I look at the bigger stones again?" Big mistake. The stones were larger, but so was the price tag.

Then I thought of a plan as brilliant as the square-cut beauty I'd chosen. "I'd really like this one," I said softly. "Suppose Bill gave you a check for four hundred and I gave you a check for the difference?"

She eyed me evenly. "Are you sure that's how you want to begin your marriage?"

Oh. Heat flew to my cheeks. "Maybe not." I turned away in embarrassment, ashamed to have my sins spread out like so many sharp stones on display. Greed, deceit, covetousness, pride—and those were just the smaller ones.

The wisdom of Proverbs 31:11 came to mind: "Her husband has full confidence in her and lacks nothing of value." Nothing except an honest wife.

I gazed at Bill across the room, a man who deserved a woman he could trust with his heart and his wallet, and silently begged his forgiveness—and God's. Thankfully, I'd been handed something more valuable than diamonds: a second chance.

When I turned back to the jeweler, we were both smiling. "You're absolutely right," I assured her. "The smaller stone will be perfect."

And so it was. Perfectly lovely. I flashed it about as though it were the Hope Diamond because for me, that's what it represented: my hopes for a marriage built on honesty, not deception, and a forever kind of love that would outshine any diamond.

For our tenth anniversary, Bill—bless his generous heart!—replaced my tiny stone with a whole band of twinkling beauties. If there are flaws, I haven't noticed them. I'm too busy whispering a prayer of thanks for the One who overlooks my flaws by the hour and polishes me clean every morning.

Liz Curtis Higgs

My Conversation with God

Praying for God to bless others can be risky.

About five years ago, my wife and I visited an elderly and very sick man who had once been our pastor. We discovered that he and his wife lived not far from us, and we renewed our old acquaintance. During one of our first visits, the man's grandsons—14-year-old twins—came for a visit. The moment I met them, an inner voice told me that someday I would play a role in one of their lives. I brushed it off as a "brain hiccup" and thought little more of it.

During the next five years, we drew closer to that family and got to know the twins well. Gradually, one of them shared with us his call to the ministry of music.

When the twins were 17, they and their parents visited us and toured the campus where I teach. The one called to music ministry was immediately struck with the impression he was to attend this particular university and none other. Over the next year, it became clearer to us that he was very serious. As far as I could tell, it had nothing to do with the fact that I teach there; he was following an inner tug of divine guidance.

But my university is expensive, and his family is of modest means. During his senior year of high school, he applied for scholarships, but the results were not encouraging. Still, his enthusiasm for studying for ministry at this university didn't flag.

I felt a strong burden to help him, but contrary to popular perception, Christian university professors are not prosperous. And my book royalties had never added up to any large amounts.

One bright and beautiful morning in October 2005, I went out alone, walking and praying. I began to cry out to God for my young friend. "Oh, God, please use me to make it possible for him to go to this university!" I don't know what I expected to happen, but I committed to letting God use me however he wanted to on this young man's behalf.

The next week, I was at the same spot in my morning exercise when something amazing happened. Out of the blue, a book title came to me. It was so clever I knew two things instantly: It wasn't mine, and it would sell.

Then, in almost the same instant, the entire outline of the book was there in my mind. Every chapter and its title. No discursive thought preceded it. I immediately went home and began writing. As I wrote, I had the distinct feeling that this was not me. I had never written like this before. The words poured out. Two weeks later, a 200-page manuscript sat on my desk. I knew it was good.

But what to do with it? I had never before written a book without a contract. As I sat and looked at the printed pages, the name of a well-known Christian book publisher suddenly came to mind. I had never dealt with the company before, but I had met the chief editor at professional society meetings. I felt directed to contact him even though I knew the publisher's procedure for considering book proposals and manuscripts was quite different and more complicated.

I sent my acquaintance an e-mail message containing the title and the outline. A day later, I received an encouraging response; he wanted to read the manuscript. So I sent it to him. Within weeks, I had a contract; it required only a little tweaking of two or three brief portions of the manuscript.

While talking to the editor assigned to this project, I discovered something astonishing. The publisher wanted to pay me a handsome royalty in advance for the book. It was approximately ten times anything I had ever received up front before. I felt as if I had won the lottery!

Later, I took another brisk walk through my neighborhood. My mind was concentrating on the financial windfall and how to use it. Coincidentally, the estimated cost of my house's much-needed roof replacement was the same as the royalty advance paid by my new publisher. The answer seemed clear—a new roof.

Then God spoke: "It's not your money."

Those were the first words of a conversation that lasted on and off for several days. Knowing instantly it wasn't a "brain hiccup" but something more real and serious, I asked, "What do you mean it's not my money?" My tone was resentful and defensive.

"It's not your money. It's his." The voice inside my head was as real as if it were audible. I knew with terrifying certainty it wasn't my imagination because I didn't want to hear it.

"Whose?" I asked.

The voice named the young man for whom I had been praying only a few weeks earlier. "It's for him to go to the university and study for the ministry."

"All of it?"

"That and the rest."

I knew "the rest" meant any further royalties the book might earn after it was published.

Absolutely flabbergasted, I raised my fist in the air and asked aloud, "What about my roof?"

The voice said, "I'll take care of your roof if you'll be obedient."

Then I said, "If you want to use me to help him go to the university, why not give me everything it will cost? Why this amount that will make a difference but not pay his whole way?"

"Others have to be obedient too," I heard in reply.

When I arrived home, I shared the conversation with my wife, who had been looking forward to a roof that wouldn't leak. I couldn't talk about it without sobbing almost uncontrollably. I was shaking with emotion. Nothing like this had ever happened to me before. My wife is more spiritual than I am. She immediately agreed; we would wait for a new roof.

Today, my young friend is living in a residence hall and taking courses, including courses in preparation for music ministry.

ANONYMOUS

Life Is Not like a VCR

Suffering sometimes brings startling clarity to life.

I've been around college students a long time, and you can't help but have your favorites. One of my favorites was a kid named Tim Vanderveen from Spring Lake, Michigan. Tall and broad shouldered with curly hair and a smile as broad as the dawn, he was as handsome as they came. He was a great student. He graduated from Hope College in the early nineties and took a job at Prince Corporation, now Johnson Controls. He scurried up the ladder of success about as quickly as anyone can. That is, until a rawboned, wind-whipped November afternoon.

I was sitting in my office, and my secretary told me Tim Vanderveen was on the line. He's a friend, so I was eager to talk to him. I said, "Hey, Tim, how you doing?"

A weak, trembling voice said, "I'm not doing so good."

I said, "What's up with you?"

He said, "I'm in the hospital in Grand Rapids. I got the flu or something. My folks are out of the country."

I said, "I'm going to be in Grand Rapids later today. Maybe I can stop by and see you. Would that be okay?"

He said, "I'd like that a lot."

By the time I got to Tim, the doctors had already been there. It wasn't the flu. It was leukemia. And that began a three-year, arduous battle that he would lose—or win, maybe.

Now come with me to room 5255 at Butterworth Hospital. They call it Spectrum Health now. I walked into the room. His mother was sitting in the corner crying. You can't blame her. Tim was lying on his side. They had positioned the pillows between his skinny little legs. His hair wasn't curly anymore. There wasn't enough energy for him to look at me, so I got down on one knee so I could look at him eyeball to eyeball. I said, "Hi, Tim." He said, "Hi, Tim." There was a long, awkward pause. I'd been a pastor for 20 years, and I still didn't know what to say. He broke the silence.

He said, "I've learned something."

Now I know this much at least: You don't trifle with the words of a person who is about to die; you just listen carefully. So I said, "Tell me, partner, what have you learned?"

He said, "I've learned that life is not like a VCR."

Now, I didn't get it then any more than you're getting it now. So I said, "I don't get it. What do you mean?"

He said, "It's not like a VCR; you can't fast-forward the bad parts." Long pause. I'm thinking to myself, *Where does he get this stuff?* Then he interrupts the silence again to say, "But I have learned that Jesus Christ is in every frame, and right now that's just enough."

It was just enough when his parents rocked that little baby at the waters of baptism that Jesus Christ should be in the frame. It was just enough when he toddled off to first grade that Jesus Christ should be in the frame. It was just enough when he turned his tassel toward an uncertain future at Hope College that Jesus Christ should be in that frame. And it was just enough when he breathed his last here and his first there that Jesus Christ should be in the frame.

Tim Brown

Garage-Sale Blues

A good deal can mean more than making money.

I parked in front of a house that was holding an indoor moving sale. The front door was open as if urging, *Come in and buy my treasures.* As I wandered through the house, searching for hidden gems, I found a case under a pile of old bedspreads in the back bedroom. Inside was a shiny saxophone, beautifully engraved with the figure of a woman. It was vintage, in pristine condition, and I bought it for only $20.

Unfamiliar with the going rate for instruments, I called my husband to do a quick eBay search. No way could I afford to end up with another white elephant to store in my shed. It was crowded enough!

I heard Rick's fingers tapping, then silence. "There aren't any listed."

Odd. It seemed to me that someone should have at least one saxophone for sale. "You're sure?"

"Not one."

I ended the call, worried. I was $20 poorer and the proud owner of a shiny saxophone that might not sell. What did I know about musical instruments? All I could play was the radio. As I was leaving, an elderly man stopped me. "May I buy that saxophone from you?" he asked hopefully. "I'll give you twenty dollars more than what you paid."

I was thrilled. I'd not only recoup my $20 but make 20 more—and within minutes of my purchase. I viewed it as God's unexpected provision, a blessing.

Later that day I sat at the computer, pulled up the eBay homepage, and entered the type of saxophone I'd owned for less than five minutes. To my horror, three exact matches popped up, all selling for more than $500. "Rick!" I wailed, pointing at the screen. "Look!"

He wrinkled his nose. "Oh."

"You said there weren't any saxophones listed!" I felt weak. I was losing consciousness.

"That's weird. When I looked there weren't any listed."

Suddenly, I realized the problem: Rick hadn't gone to the eBay homepage; he'd gone to my seller's page. Of course I didn't have a sax listed. I had an enamel coffeepot with no bids, a sunbonnet girl quilt with no bids, and a primitive cabinet, also without a bid. I'd sold the sax cheap. God wanted to bless me abundantly, but I'd blown it! It was as if someone had snatched money right out of my pocket, and I'd let it happen.

It was done. Finished. No chance for a do-over. Yet I couldn't let it go. Late at night I sat sleepless, angry with myself for harboring ill feelings. My brain kept replaying the moment I sold the sax while a bitter little voice whispered that the old man had probably pawned it. I felt envious, consumed by greed—and guilty. God was revealing a side of me that I hadn't known existed.

I opened my Bible to Galatians 6: "Let us not become weary in doing good, for at the proper time we will reap a harvest if we do not give up." Next I turned to my concordance and made note cards of ten verses about praising God. Each time I thought about the sax, I lifted my arms and praised God, thanking him and quoting Scripture. "Give thanks in all circumstances, for this is God's will for you" (1 Thessalonians 5:18). I was amazed by how my turmoil fled, leaving behind pure happiness. I was set free, and once more my life became enjoyable. I even let Rick off the hook, so his life became enjoyable as well!

A few months later as I was perusing a garage sale, I spied my sax buyer hunched over a box, sifting through old sheet music. Feeling the old twinge of regret, I pretended not to see him. But he recognized me and cheerfully called out, "Hello there! Have you found any treasures today?"

"No."

As I turned to walk away, he caught hold of my arm. "I want you to know that because of your spontaneous generosity, I rekindled my old passion for the saxophone. Being retired, I now volunteer my time to teach kids how to play." He wiggled his fingers over the keys of an invisible sax. It was then I noticed his frailty, his worn clothes, and his scuffed shoes.

And suddenly I understood. I thought he'd stolen my blessing, when in fact he was my blessing. God's provision is for us all. And I was blessed to have received it twice, and in the most unusual place.

I'd call that a double blessing.

ROBIN LEE SHOPE

Thy Kingdom Come

Why repentance is always good news.

The movie *The Soloist* tells the story of the friendship between Nathaniel Ayers, a homeless man with an undiagnosed mental illness, and Steven Lopez, a *Los Angeles Times* columnist. In one scene Steven spends the night on the streets with Nathaniel. Rats scurry around them on the street as people weep, laugh, brawl, jabber, stagger, and embrace. They curl up in sleeping bags, huddle in stairwells, hunker down over meals. Meanwhile, Nathaniel recites the Lord's Prayer. His voice floats over the street's madness and tenderness, its beauty and squalor. "Thy kingdom come," Nathaniel says, and a woman screams at a man, flailing her fists at his chest. "Thy will be done," he says, and two men share a cigarette. "On earth as it is in heaven," as a church group hands out boxed meals.

We're left to ponder—is Nathaniel asking for the kingdom to come to these streets, or is he announcing that the kingdom is already present? Wheat growing beside tares, pearls buried in stony fields, glory hidden in clay jars?

Jesus said to the questioning Pharisees, "The kingdom of God is within you," but they never managed to see it. Jesus, King of kings, stood before them. The kingdom was among them, and they nailed it to a cross.

To see the kingdom, to open your heart and eyes to it, you must repent. Jesus's inaugural address was exactly that. "The time has come," he said. "The kingdom of God is near. Repent and believe the good news."

Repentance is not a popular idea anymore. That's a loss, because

Jesus connects repentance with both his kingdom and his gospel. At the church where I pastor, we talk a lot about both—the kingdom and the gospel. And so we've learned to talk often about repentance as well. It is, after all, the narrow door into the big kingdom.

But I don't take the old fire-and-brimstone approach, scowling, thundering, finger waving. I doubt Jesus struck that pose. Jesus's message is not, "Repent because hell looms close." His message is, "Repent because the kingdom is near." There's a world of difference between the two. In Jesus's hands repentance is an invitation, not a threat. It's a promise, not a curse. It's good news, not bad. Repentance often involves sorrow. But it's sorrow that quickly turns to gladness because repentance is the gift of starting fresh. It's the doorway into life abundant, life anew, and life eternal. Repentance means that what I've done and who I am no longer need define me. My past is not my destiny unless I choose to let it be.

So almost weekly, I ask people to repent. I ask them to change their minds, which is literally what repentance means. I invite them to see things God's way. To align themselves, stem to stern, with God's purposes. Initially that alignment is violent and dramatic, a 180-degree turn. But thereafter it's mostly course corrections—15 degrees here, 5 degrees there.

But every turn, by whatever degree, is good news. Every turn moves us closer to where we want to be.

I'm thinking of Muriel. Muriel's childhood crippled her emotionally. She began visits to the hospital's psychiatric ward when she was in her teens. By her late forties, she'd seen dozens of counselors, therapists, and psychiatrists. She was on a cocktail of anti-this and anti-that medications potent enough to subdue a blue whale. She had logged no fewer than 61 rounds of electric shock therapy. But nothing really helped.

The problem was what others had done to her: cruel things, malicious things, godless things. Did she need to repent? Hardly. They did. But they wouldn't.

One day she walked into the office of a new therapist. Muriel was cynical. She had low expectations. The therapist heard her story, and simply asked a question: "How would your life have been different if someone had come alongside you when you were 14 and showed you your strengths instead of telling you that you were sick?"

"In all those years," she said, "I'd never considered that. And then I saw it: I wasn't stuck in my life as I knew it. My life could be otherwise. I decided then and there to live it otherwise. I changed my mind about who I was, which allowed me to change everything almost instantly."

In a word, she repented. You should see her now. The kingdom has come.

Mark Buchanan

White as Snow

*Was Glorianna really the right person to play the
angel in this year's Christmas pageant?*

"So, is tonight when you turn into an angel?" Beth asked as she held
up her friend Glory's flowing white costume. Beth propped the sanctuary door open with one hip as she ran her fingers over the diaphanous
fabric. "Heavenly," she commented. "Maybe we should post a sign out
front: *Live Angels—One Night Only.*"

"Works for me," Glory replied as she breezed through the doorway.
With a brief flashback to Christmases past, she added over her shoulder, "Anything's better than *Girls! Girls! Girls!*"

Their laughter echoed among the empty pews of Chesapeake Community Church as Glory made her way down the aisle toward the
dressing room behind the choir loft. Having Beth for a friend was like
celebrating Christmas every day of the year. Beth was funny and honest,
and the girl knew how to listen. Over the last year, Glory had talked—
a *lot*—and Beth had listened, nodded, and offered wise counsel. Now
that the worst was over, they'd become simply friends. Glory took turns
listening and, when she felt brave, threw in a word of encouragement.

*Glorianna Wilson giving spiritual advice? Talk about your basic
miracle.*

She walked into the chilly dressing room and hung her costume on
a rack crammed with old choir robes. "The ghosts of Christmas past,"
she murmured, glancing at a pile of dusty shepherds' tunics and faded
crowns from long-forgotten magi.

If she thought about the Christmases she'd missed over the last
few years, her costume would be soaked with tears. "You're here *this*

Christmas," she reminded herself aloud, staring at the bright mirror edged with lights. "Today is what matters, Glory."

She slipped out of her sweater and jeans, hands shivering as she unwrapped the plastic around her angelic costume. White tights and a leotard came first. Nice, heavyweight material, she was relieved to discover. The more coverage, the better. The bold design of a lily on her thigh, compliments of Tattoo Charlie's, disappeared without a trace beneath the stretchy tights.

Rather than a stiff pair of wings, the costume had layers of white chiffon that floated around her when she moved. She eased the tealength dress over her head and let it fall into place on her shoulders. *Perfect.* Lifting her hands above her head, she spun and swayed to an imaginary tune, thrilled to see how gracefully the gauzy material followed her every move.

Glorianna Wilson, an angel? Yet another miracle.

She was digging around in her purse for a brush when a knock at the door startled her.

"It's me, Glory." It was Beth's voice. "Are you dressed? Pastor Miller is looking for you. Says he'd like to see you in his office."

Glory peeked around the edge of the door, her heart in her throat. "Is there a problem?"

Beth shrugged. "He didn't say, but I wouldn't worry about it. I'll tell him you'll be there in a couple minutes." She winked. "You look great, hon."

Hurrying to finish, Glory brushed her pale hair into a simple French braid, and then she removed every bit of makeup until she was white as snow from her blond head to the toes of her new ballet slippers. *Clean. Pure.* Not innocent, though. She could never be that. But she was forgiven. That's what Beth kept telling her: "That old you is *gone*, Glory. Your sins are forgiven, your past is forgotten, and you're brand-new. Trust me."

She was learning to trust, but it was a slow process. Over the years, she'd made the mistake of trusting people who intentionally robbed her of everything that mattered most: her identity, her dignity, her sense of self-worth. Her old stage name—*Starlight*—was an ironic choice, considering she was surrounded by darkness.

When a high school friend had dragged her to Chesapeake Community Church ten months ago, Glory never could have imagined the changes that would take place—first in her heart and then in her life.

Trying out for the pageant was a huge step. The director, watching her dance across the platform and down the aisle, had pronounced Glory a natural.

Right.

She smiled at her image in the mirror now, her lips trembling. *Let them praise his name with dancing.* When she'd found that verse in Psalms last week, she'd wept for an hour. To think of dancing for *God*!

Glory took a steadying breath and then left the cluttered room behind and padded down the carpeted hallway with floor-to-ceiling windows that looked into various church offices. Chesapeake was one of Baltimore County's fastest-growing congregations. She'd connected with only a handful of people so far, taking her time to get to know them before they found out too much about her. It was safer that way.

Pastor Ron Miller, standing at his office door, waved her toward him. Through the glass, she could see a group of men surrounding his desk. "Some of the elders," he explained in a low voice. "Everything will be fine, Glory. I promise. C'mon in."

An invisible knot tightened inside her. It didn't *feel* fine. Their faces were solemn, their postures stiff. Disapproval hung in the air.

Ron patted the back of his leather desk chair. "Sit here, Glorianna." He'd used her proper name. Not a good sign. Moving behind her, he folded his arms over his chest. "Now, gentlemen. You were saying?"

The men—half a dozen, mostly middle-aged—looked at each other, shifted in their chairs, but said nothing. Finally, one man in a striped sweater cleared his throat. "I want to know what you're going to do about this Christmas pageant, Ron."

"I'm going to attend, that's what." Pastor Miller's words bore the hint of a smile. "My wife's already bought our tickets for tonight. Do you fellas need seats?"

The man's chin jutted out. "That's not what I'm asking, and you know it." He looked directly at Glory. "Did you know about…about this young woman?"

"What do I need to know, Jack?"

"She used to be a…" He glanced at the others for support. "An 'exotic dancer.' Worked at one of those clubs on the Block, downtown on Baltimore Street."

A wave of heat traveled up Glory's neck and across her cheeks. *The Block*. Adult bookstores and peepshow booths, pornography shops and filthy strip joints, the Charm City Lounge among them. If Pastor Miller's hand hadn't lightly rested on her shoulder, she might have bolted from the room in shame.

Another elder spoke up. "I'm not sure it's wise to have Glory dancing in our Christmas pageant." His voice was sharp, accusing. "When did you know about this situation?"

"I've always known, Phil. Just like I know about your—uh, situation." The pastor walked around to the front of his desk as though to protect her. "And yours, Carl." He nodded at one of the younger men, whose face surely was redder than her own. "And yours, Steve."

Silence hung over the room. When Pastor Miller spoke again, his words were tender and utterly without judgment. "The fact is, Mary, the mother of Jesus, had a reputation too. When word got around that she was pregnant out of wedlock…well, you can be sure there was talk, not all of it kind."

He eyed Glory for a moment and then turned back to the elders, who looked duly chastised. "I know Mary was an innocent young woman, and the old Glorianna Wilson wasn't. But when Glory gave her life to Christ last January, and he told her to leave her life of sin, well…" He glanced at her angelic attire, a broad smile across his face. "She did."

Jack sputtered, "But what if someone at *The Sun* finds out? We've got a reporter who comes to the second service. You don't want something like this all over the news."

Pastor Miller scratched his head in mock confusion. "Isn't sharing the good news the whole idea, Jack?" One of the others chuckled, and the atmosphere in the room grew noticeably lighter. "Glory's a great example of what this church is all about: hope and grace, not fear and condemnation. I can't think of anyone better suited for the part."

When Ron opened his office door, Glory realized the pageant rehearsal was already in full swing across the hall. Voices in harmony floated into the room. "That's my cue," she whispered as she made a dash for the door.

Behind her, the pastor swept the elders into the hall like a dusting of snow from his front steps. "Merry Christmas, fellas. See you at the pageant."

Michael Anderson hadn't darkened the door of a church in years, let alone one as big as Chesapeake Community. He sat in the last pew, feeling awkward and out of place. Whose idea was this, anyway? *Courtney's.*

He glanced at the dark-haired beauty next to him and folded his hand around hers. He'd waited a long time to find someone this nice. If Courtney wanted him to go to a Christmas pageant, fine. Whatever. As long as he was with her, he was happy.

The place didn't look anything like a church. A huge stage set filled the front and sides, painted with tents and palm trees. He didn't know much about the Bible, but he figured it must be Bethlehem. "O Little Town of…" and all that.

As the lights dimmed and orchestral music filled the air, a woman playing the role of Mary came out on stage, and an angel appeared with an announcement. "You're pregnant." Michael shook his head, feeling sorry for poor Joseph.

Another woman walked onstage, decidedly expectant. Michael tipped his head toward Courtney's. "Who's that?"

"Elizabeth," she whispered back. "The mother-to-be of John the Baptist."

He nodded, hoping she didn't realize he was clueless when it came to that stuff.

While Mary sang, a woman dressed in white swirled onto the stage. Not dancing, exactly—more like floating. Michael sat up straighter, craning his neck for a better look. Was she supported by wires?

Her white dress was made of clouds, her feet had wings. While

Mary sang, "My soul glorifies the Lord, and my spirit rejoices in God my Savior," the dancer rejoiced all around her, not with words, but with movement.

He nudged Courtney, his gaze glued to the stage. "Who's the dancer?"

"I don't know," she murmured. "Isn't she glorious?"

Yeah, that was a good word: *glorious*. Her dancing was almost holy. Like a real angel had come to earth.

Too bad he hadn't steered Courtney closer to the front where he could see the dancer's face. Even from here, he could tell she was something to see. Not that he was attracted to her. It was more like he was *drawn* to her. Something about her innocence tugged at his insides.

That didn't make sense. He was anything but innocent.

Wait…She was gliding down the steps toward the aisle. Michael swallowed an uneasy lump in his throat. He sat, eyes transfixed, as she spun closer, bending low to touch the floor and then sweeping her arms up, up toward the heavens.

But it was her face that undid him.

No makeup, no lipstick. No color except the clear blue of her eyes. She glowed as if she'd swallowed a star and it shone through her skin. What *was* this woman's story? How could anyone be so transparent?

She was right next to him now, oblivious to the crowd, her thoughts apparently elsewhere. As she swung in a slow circle, he looked at her face and their eyes met, just for a brief moment.

I know her! Michael thought.

But that was impossible. He shook his head as though some puzzle piece might fall into place. How could he know her? Courtney was the first churchgoing chick he'd dated since…well, since forever.

He glanced over his shoulder, his gaze following the dancer out the back door of the sanctuary. Maybe she'd appear again later and dance her way back down the aisle. She was vaguely familiar, though nothing he could pin down. Not somebody from work. A waitress, maybe?

He waited through the long program, glancing over his shoulder now and again, hoping she'd make a second appearance. Familiar carols he hadn't heard in years filled him with a forgotten joy. He squeezed Courtney's hand more than once just to feel the warmth of it. He hadn't thought this much about Christmas for a long time.

When live camels with three wise men showed up onstage, he was so distracted by the spectacle, he almost missed seeing the blonde dancer slip into the pew across the aisle from him.

No more white costume. Jeans and a bright red sweater now. Her hair fell across her shoulders. And she had makeup on. Not much, but a little. Red lipstick, to match her sweater.

Maybe it was a coincidence, or maybe she sensed him staring at her. She turned directly toward him and met his gaze head-on.

And then he knew. Knew where he'd met her, why she looked familiar. The Charm City Lounge. Last year over the holidays, he and some buddies from work went there on a dare. The place was dark and dirty, the liquor watered down, the music too loud, the girls hard-looking. Their bodies were inviting, but their eyes were vacant.

And this woman, this leggy blonde, had been among them. He remembered her, not because she was prettier than the rest, but because there was something different about her. She hadn't looked tough; she'd looked broken.

He studied her out of the corner of his eye. She didn't look broken now. Just the opposite. Maybe his memory was playing tricks on him.

When the last chord rang through the sanctuary, followed by thunderous applause, Michael rose to his feet along with everyone else, clapping with more sincerity than he'd felt in ages.

Courtney touched his arm. "Michael, do you mind if I step backstage for a second and say hi to one of my friends in the choir? I won't be long."

"No problem." Perfect, in fact. He'd been trying to figure out how he could catch the dancer before she left and not hurt Courtney's feelings. "I'll be right here, babe."

Courtney's dark head barely had disappeared into the crowd when he turned to find the dancer a footstep away, looking directly at him. Waiting for him, almost.

"Glorianna Wilson," she said in a soft voice, extending her hand to shake his. "My friends call me Glory. I noticed you were staring at me and thought we might have met."

He was speechless. It *was* her, no question. "We did. Sort of. Not… uh…" He glanced at the rows of pews and racks of Bibles. "Not here, though."

She tipped her head to the side, eyeing him with amusement. "At the Lounge?"

He poked at the carpeting with his toe. "Yeah." Those blue eyes saw too much. "How'd you recognize me?"

"Oh, I didn't recognize you at all." She shrugged. "After a while, you know the look. Men used to pass me on the street, do a double take, that kind of thing."

"Uh-huh." Overcome with curiosity, Michael lifted his chin and tried not to stare. "It *is* you, then? I can't believe you're the same woman."

"I'm not." Her radiant smile transformed her face. The dancer from the Lounge was gone.

"What…?" Michael searched for the right word. "What happened?"

"Christmas happened." Her smile turned to laughter, ringing like sleigh bells. "Easter happened. Jesus came to earth a baby, and he rose from earth a Savior. He lived and died and lives again for me. And for you." Her words were gentle. "What's your name, by the way?"

"Michael."

"Ah." She nodded, obviously pleased. "Like the angel."

"Listen." He leaned closer, keeping his voice low. "Aren't you afraid someone might recognize you?"

She leaned closer too. "Someone has."

"Oh."

Slowly straightening, she looked at him as though she could see right through his tough skin. "Michael, you watched me dance once. But God watched me dance every night. I didn't know it then, but he was right there with me, waiting for me to open my eyes and see the truth."

Michael shook his head, confused by her confidence. "But don't people think less of you, once they know?"

Her shining hair framed her face like a halo. "I don't mind if people think less of me. Maybe they'll think more of God."

When someone called her name, she turned to go. "Merry Christmas, Michael. I hope I'll see you here again."

By the time he could say what was on his heart, she'd started down the aisle. "I think you will, Glorianna," he called after her. "And... Merry Christmas!"

Liz Curtis Higgs

New Shoes

Can a pair of shoes help a kid learn to make smart choices?

A few weeks after I began pastoring Messiah Presbyterian Church in Lubbock, Texas, I heard a teacher from a nearby elementary school tell about a boy in his class who was a lookout for a drug dealer. The child was from a poor family, but now he was wearing expensive athletic shoes. The teacher was concerned. "What can I do with this kid?" he asked. "He's only seven years old. He doesn't understand what he's doing. He thinks he's making a good choice when he's making a bad one."

That week, I met with the six elders of my church. I told them about the boy at the school, and I proposed we help by supplying an incentive for kids to make right choices instead of wrong ones.

My proposal was that Messiah Church offer three kids in each classroom each semester a pair of the best athletic shoes money could buy if they made right choices by excelling in school. The school had 17 classrooms, so that would come to 51 pairs of shoes a semester—102 pairs a year. It could cost us as much as $10,000.

They were silent. I knew very well we did not have the money. "We will raise the money," I said. *Ten thousand dollars.*

I knew what they were thinking. Messiah had a tiny budget, and there were times when the utility bills could hardly be paid.

"We should pray," Bettie struggled to say. After praying, we looked up and saw Bettie's eyes were bright.

"I think the Lord means for us to do this," Don said. The others agreed.

This is not one of those stories in which we immediately went to the mailbox and found a check for $10,000. Still, when I mentioned it to various friends and community contacts, many wrote checks for $100 or $300.

We called FootLocker and Kids FootLocker, and they thought it was such a wonderful idea, they promised an initial discount of 15 percent and 25 percent at the respective stores.

We announced the honors during a school assembly at the end of the first semester. "Everybody around here knows you can make a lot of money doing the wrong thing," I said to the children. "But these shoes are for kids choosing to do the right thing. In the end, more good will come to you for making right choices. We are here to show you that is true. When you go into FootLocker or Kids FootLocker, pick out any pair of shoes you want—any pair—because you have done the right thing. Everyone who does the right thing is a winner!"

A week later, one of the sixth-grade teachers told me that after the assembly, the other kids in her classroom said to the winners, "You just wait. When you get into that shoe store, you won't be able to get whatever you want. They'll just give you some cheap, junky shoe."

That afternoon and evening, 40 of the 50 winners went to the mall to get their shoes. The FootLocker managers told me each child who came in had the same question: "Can I get anything I want? *Anything?*" The managers replied as we had asked them to: "Yes you can, because you are a winner." That next day in school, the principal said her office was nearly overrun with kids who wanted to show her their wonderful new shoes. She said the whole school was in celebration.

PAMELA BAKER POWELL

The Vision Thing

Clarity came just as things got blurry.

My vision has never been good. I've worn eyeglasses since second grade and contact lenses since high school. Once during a Little League game, a line drive smacked me right on the nose, splitting my glasses' plastic frames neatly in half. My vision was so bad that at optometrists' exams, the only letter I could see on the eye chart was the big E—and then only because I knew it was an E.

For several years, I pondered whether I should have laser surgery to correct my vision. Friends and colleagues gave the procedure glowing reviews, and I read positive testimonies on websites and blogs. My main stumbling block was justifying the cost. Was it a vanity expense, like a face-lift or a tummy tuck? But after losing yet another contact, I calculated that I'd spent enough money on lost lenses, contact fluid, and other supplies, and it might be better stewardship to get my vision corrected.

Last year, I took the plunge. Encouraged by a coupon given to me by a friend, I went ahead and had the surgery. My corneas were too thin for the normal slice-a-flap procedure, so I underwent a different procedure (which was more expensive, of course).

It didn't quite take. The doctor said that when you throw a football from 50 yards, it's harder to be on target than it is from 5 yards. My vision had been something like 20/400, and he was able to bring it to 20/40—tantalizingly close to clear vision, but still fuzzy.

The doctor scheduled follow-up "enhancement" procedures. For the next several months, my vision remained in an in-between state, far better than it had been for decades but still not quite as sharp as I would have liked. I sat closer to my computer screen and increased the zoom on Microsoft Word to 125 percent. When I spoke at a conference, my notes were punched up to a 16-point font size.

Then I happened to attend an InterVarsity Asian-American staff conference. During corporate worship, I squinted to make out worship song lyrics on the far wall. In one particular session, we sang "God of Justice," a prayer for empowerment to feed the hungry and stand beside the broken.

I closed my eyes as we repeated the chorus, praying that God would direct me. How might I move into action? I live in such a cerebral world of books and ideas—what might I do to become more active in pursuing global mission?

The song cycled back to an earlier verse, and I opened my watering eyes. The lyrics on the screen shimmered slightly and then came crisply into focus.

I could see. Clearly. Wow—I could read every word easily without squinting!

Had God just healed me? My innards fluttered, and I suddenly understood all those clichés about feeling your heart race and pound. Had I just experienced a miracle?

I blinked several times, and my vision wavered back and forth. Clear, blurry, clear, blurry. Then I realized what was happening. While singing I had been tearing up, moved by God's call, and the thin layer of water on my eyeballs functioned like contact lenses. The tears had been making my vision clearer.

I immediately asked a friend to pray with me for clarity of vision, both literally and spiritually. There is so much I do not see. I am blind to the needs of my neighbors down the block and around the world. I do not see the plight of the enslaved child laborer, the trapped sex worker, the communities wracked by AIDS or genocide, the people around the world who still lack witness to the gospel.

I do not act because I do not see. I am blinded by insularity, privilege, and affluence, which give me the luxury of having laser surgery when countless millions around the world lack basic medical care. But when God moves me to tears, I begin to see more clearly. And I have a clearer vision for how he calls me to participate in his work as an agent of shalom at home and around the world.

I've now had follow-up enhancements on my eyes, and my vision clocks in at 20/20 for each individual eye and 20/15 when using them together. I'm grateful. But I hope that God will continue to make my eyes water for the sake of his kingdom. I suspect that I will never see as clearly as I do when I have tears in my eyes.

ALᴇHSU

The Concert of the Year

A diverse gathering at the Strathmore Music Center
experiences a spontaneous outbreak of unashamed joy.

After almost three hours, it was time for a curtain call—one last bow to end the evening's awards presentation. As the host of the event reintroduced everyone, the featured jazz band played "When the Saints Go Marching In." That's when something happened. The audience at the Strathmore rose to its feet to acknowledge the fellowship winners—it seemed at the time like one last blast of applause before the exit. But as everyone clapped in time to the music, the performers onstage began to dance.

The jazz band, sensing something in the air, got louder and kept playing. And playing. And playing. Onstage, the performers formed a conga line, led by one of the jazz musicians, and then a circle, each person taking his or her turn in the center. The invisible line between performers and audience evaporated. It had turned into one big party—or a revival meeting.

The spiritual writer Stephen Mitchell once described a holy joy "so large that it is no longer inside of you, but you are inside of it." I used to work at a record store and wrote music reviews for newspapers and websites, and I've been to hundreds of concerts over the years. I have never seen anything like what happened on that stage at the Strathmore. It was the most unself-conscious explosion of bliss I have ever seen in performance; the people onstage were not hamming for the crowd or blowing kisses. They were as lost in abandon as we were. I wouldn't be surprised if they had forgotten we were there. This was a spontaneous eruption of happiness.

Finally, the host decided that plenty of saints had marched in, and he shut things down. No one wanted to leave; I honestly believe the band could have played for an hour and no one would have moved for the exits. Staggering outside, I heard a woman say she was "swimming in joy." I myself was speechless. Then I heard someone say, "I hope someone from the media was there." I thought of saying that I was in the media. But then I had the decency to admit there were times when language failed. Like everyone else, I just wanted to stay inside the joy.

MARK GAUVREAU JUDGE

A Prayer in the Operating Room

A boy shares his deepest concern just before his surgery.

In the fall of 2005, my nine-year-old son, Austin, had his tonsils removed. Before the surgery, an anesthesiologist came in to start an IV. He was wearing a cool surgical cap covered in colorful frogs. Austin loved that frog hat. When the doctor started to leave, Austin called out, "Hey, wait."

The doctor turned. "Yeah, buddy, what do you need?"

"Do you go to church?"

"No," the doctor admitted. "I know I probably should, but I don't."

Austin then asked, "Well, are you saved?"

Chuckling nervously, the doctor said: "Nope. But after talking to you, maybe it's something I should consider."

Pleased with his response, Austin answered, "Well, you should, 'cause Jesus is great!"

"I'm sure he is, little guy," the doctor said as he quickly made his exit.

When Austin's surgery was finished, the anesthesiologist came into the waiting room to talk to me. He told me the surgery went well, and then he said, "Mrs. Blessit, I don't usually come down and talk to the parents after a surgery, but I just had to tell you what your son did."

Oh boy, I thought. *What did that little rascal do now?* The doctor explained that he'd just put the mask on Austin when my son signaled that he needed to say something. When the doctor removed the mask, Austin blurted, "Wait a minute, we have to pray!" The doctor told him to go ahead, and Austin prayed: "Dear Lord, please let all the doctors and nurses have a good day. And Jesus, please let the doctor with the frog hat get saved and start going to church. Amen."

The doctor admitted that this had touched him. "I was so sure he would pray that his surgery went well," he explained. "But he didn't even mention his surgery. He prayed for me! Mrs. Blessit, I had to come down and let you know what a great little guy you have."

A few minutes later, a nurse came to take me to post-op. She had a big smile on her face as we walked to the elevator. "There's something you should know," she said. "Some of the other nurses and I have been witnessing to that doctor and praying for him for a long time. After your son's surgery, he tracked a few of us down to tell us about Austin's prayer. He said, 'Well girls, you got me. If that little boy could pray for me when he was about to have surgery, then I think maybe I need his Jesus too.'"

TINA BLESSIT

Two Kinds of Thanks

Some things are more important—and more
secure—than our own comfort.

Spending an evening at a shelter for homeless women was not my idea, but when a friend asked, I was perfectly willing to tag along.

Although the winter was still young, the cold was harsh. I nearly ran from the comfort of our car to the warmth of the church annex that had opened its doors for years as a refuge from the night.

The director, Christy, efficiently assigned tasks—setting the floor with foam mats and blankets as one would set a table, and laying out plastic forks, paper plates, and donated leftovers on a buffet table. When the women arrived, we would help serve the food.

Christy assured me that most of the women, the regulars, had spent the day inside at one of several centers, but there were always a few who just appeared, seeming to have no history other than their names.

My three hours at the shelter were not filled with dramatic scenes. From a corner of the large sleeping area, I helped serve dinner to 30 women who ate their substantial but bland meal while they sat cross-legged on their sleeping mats. Except for two boisterously irrational women, they talked little. By nine o'clock, many were bedding down for the night.

Homeless. As I did the dishes, still within sight of the women, the word took on a personal meaning. These women slept here, but every morning when they left, they had to carry their possessions with them.

Suddenly I was overwhelmed with gratitude for my nightgowns, for my very own pillow, for my handpicked dining room chairs. *Lord,*

I silently prayed as I walked to Christy's office to say goodnight, *thank you. Thank you that I'm not one of them.*

Christy met me in the hallway and interrupted my pharisaical thoughts with her own gratitude for my help. I asked her about certain women who had caught my attention.

Rowdy Rachel, Christy explained, had a PhD in art history. Gradually her mind had slipped out of her own grasp. Esther, who had talked to herself all evening, was the mother of five children. She was a Midwestern farmer's wife—until her life crumbled around her. Christy didn't know much about Carol, who had lain on her back for more than an hour, reading her King James Bible. Marla, who had seemed sullen, was a trained soprano who occasionally enjoyed serenading the rest of the group.

Only after I walked back out into the night air did the women's stories unsettle me. Their paths had too much in common with mine. In a sense, I *was* one of them: A mother's daughter. Vulnerable. A sinner in need of grace.

Since then I have been more aware of the uprooted Vietnamese, Cambodian, and Latin American refugees who live in my neighborhood, who ride my bus. War, political change, economic collapse—conditions over which they had no control—destroyed their lifestyles and stole their ability to communicate easily and thus to work efficiently. My thoughts have frightened me. My comfortable world, my secure home, is not guaranteed.

I have always grown uncomfortable at the sight of the outstretched hand of a city beggar. Until recently, I have thought it was because of Jesus's warning in Matthew 25:45: "Whatever you did not do for one of the least of these [the hungry, thirsty, unclothed, or homeless], you did not do for me."

But since I spent an evening at the women's shelter, I see that Matthew 25 is only part of the cause of my discomfort. I am uncomfortable because I see the beggar as myself—or my very own brother or mother or father. And I cannot think of a homeless or hungry woman in such personal terms without a reversal in the way I give my thanks.

The difference between "Thank you that I'm not one of them" and

"Thank you for the grace you have shown to me, and help me to mirror your grace to others" may at first seem slight. But the second is for me a wholly new mindset. It makes me want to reach out, it reduces my discomfort around those who have less than I do, and surprisingly, it reduces my fear of a future that is unknown. Why? Because even though I know I have no insurance policy against war and famine or sickness, I know I have a God who does not forget his own. And for that I thank him also.

EVELYN BENCE

A Pleasing Decision

Choices and relationships often go hand in hand.

Recently, I was doing some light shopping at our local grocery store. After picking up some staples, I headed to the all-important potato-chip aisle. Unlike my usual routine, I had already decided what kind of chips I wanted to buy. With my eyes set like flint, I walked unflinchingly down the center of the aisle, ignoring the siren calls of all the competing brands, until I stopped in front of the Mikesell's chip display.

As soon as I picked out two sharp-looking bags, I heard a familiar voice behind me: "Way to go, Van! Thanks a lot, buddy." It was my friend Chuck, a member of the congregation I pastor—and a deliveryman for Mikesell's!

Now, imagine how I would have felt if Chuck had seen me hugging a seductive bag of Ruffles. But there's a reason that he didn't. About 30 minutes earlier, I had run into Chuck at the local bakery. He and I spent a few minutes talking together, and then we each went our way. When I arrived at the grocery store and began considering what chips to buy, I remembered that Chuck worked for Mikesell's and would probably be pleased if I purchased the brand he sold. The time we had just spent together influenced my choice.

The whole experience reminded me of something important: Spending time with my heavenly Father and being reminded of what pleases him will likely result in my decisions being more pleasing to him. Perhaps I'll even get a "Way to go, Van!"

Van Morris

A Valentine's Day Dilemma

*What kind of valentine is a young boy to give
to someone who has hurt him so badly?*

One night after supper, my son Chase sat down in the living room to sign and seal the Valentine's Day cards he had picked out for his second-grade classmates. Seeing him surrounded by mountains of cards, envelopes, and a list of names that filled an entire page, I decided to enter into the spirit of the holiday and give him a hand.

"Here, you can seal the cards and mark the names off the list," he said, shoving 15 or more cards and envelopes into my lap.

I set my coffee down on a coaster and began stuffing cards into their proper envelopes. About halfway through the stack I noticed a bold red and pink valentine inscribed with the words, "I am thankful for you." What caught my eye was not what the card said but the thick black lines that had been scrawled over the word *thankful*.

I nudged Chase and said, "I don't think it would be very kind to give this card to one of your friends."

I was not prepared for the angry outburst that followed. Chase sat up straight and yelled, "Every day that girl calls me names, and I asked her to stop, but she just laughs and curses at me!"

My heart felt a lurch of pain as I pictured Chase standing undefended in the schoolyard with this unknown girl teasing him. I sat and took in the tears that were rolling down Chase's face. I told him how sorry I was and that I could understand why he felt so hurt.

Chase jerked himself loose from my arm and with a fresh flow of tears choked out, "She embarrasses me! Do you want me to just stand there and let her call me names?"

My young son was facing a moment of suffering that might seem small to some but was clearly a big deal to him. What did I want Chase to learn about suffering in this moment?

I put my arm around Chase, wiped his tears with a Kleenex, and said, "Yes, Chase, I do want you to let her call you names. I don't want you to do anything that would hurt her."

I continued to hold him as he calmed down and thought about his choice. After a few moments, he slowly picked up a new card and addressed it neatly to this girl who so easily hurt his heart. His choice was to offer her forgiveness and grace in the form of a Valentine's card.

SONYA REEDER

When God Interrupts

God displays his presence in surprising places.

The way pastors work, we easily confuse an outboard motor for the wind of the Spirit. We are God-called but task-driven. We find ourselves up to our eyebrows in earthbound pursuits: drafting worship plans, writing memos, reading minutes, sorting mail, phoning cantankerous parishioners.

In the wake of our religious activity, God gets pushed to the periphery.

I want to be Moses, but I feel like Aaron. I'm the one down in the valley managing camp life. Mount Sinai's lofty crags are someone else's reality. Pastoral work becomes boring, predictable, routine.

Where's the lightning, fire, wind, voice…where is God?

Then I visit Mary.

Today is the first time I will see her in her new home. Just a few days earlier, she was moved from the hospital to this nursing home, a move she dreaded, a move she fought tooth and nail. Mary never planned to spend her golden years in a nursing home.

Providence has turned the tables on Mary. Her stroke partially paralyzed one side of her body. Nor can she speak the way she wants to. A woman used to serving others is forced to swallow her pride. She must learn to receive. Even in this bustling center of geriatric care, she sits alone in her wheelchair, isolated from family and friends.

As I walk down the hallways of the nursing home, my eyes search for her familiar face. There she is.

"Well, Mary!" I holler.

Mary turns her head: "Oooooh, my friend!" Bright smile. Twin-kling eyes. Warm hug.

In this unguarded moment, Mary's speech is clear. It's when she tries the hardest that things get garbled. Now Mary desperately wants to talk but can't. Her desperation only makes her more frustrated. After a few attempts at a conversation, I suggest we wander down to the activity center.

"I have a gift for you, Mary."

Several years ago Mary gave me a gift—her poetry. Mary's poetry is not merely a collection of pretty verses but an expression of heartfelt devotion to Jesus, a window into a saint at prayer.

Today I want to return the gift. I can't give Mary her speech back, but I can give her the gift of memory.

Her eyes betray her eagerness as I open the envelope, and I begin to read the first poem. After just a few words, her eyes brighten, she leans forward, and a question forms on her lips.

"Yes, it's yours," I say.

Mary smiles and then laughs.

"It's good, isn't it?" I say, and she giggles like a schoolgirl.

"Yes, it's good, Mary!"

For the next half hour, we read her poem-prayers together and laugh and worship. Surrounded by wheelchairs and white hair, lone-liness and boredom, we roar and giggle and feel the presence of Jesus.

Down here in the valley, among the ordinary tasks of the day, today a bit of heaven opens up. God meets us ordinary people in an ordi-nary place.

How easily I forget.

CHRIS ERDMAN

A Divine Calculation

I knew that God would answer my prayer, but
he had only 30 minutes to do it.

Time was running out. I needed $153.27 by two p.m., and it was already one thirty. I was confident that God would meet my need for this amount when the time came, but this was cutting it awfully close.

I sat in my car outside a restaurant where I had just eaten lunch with several ladies from my church. When it came time to pay for the meal, I picked up the tab of a guest missionary from Romania, using my last $20.

God will provide my need, I said confidently to myself. But my certainty began to waver as the breeze blew through my car windows. No one else knew about my dilemma.

What should I do? Keys still clutched in my hand, I laid my head back against the headrest and thought of Matthew 17:27. Jesus's disciples needed money to pay their taxes. He told them to go to the lake, and the first fish they caught would have a coin in its mouth that would cover the amount they needed.

"Dear Lord," I prayed. "I need a fish soon. Please show me where to find the lake."

There was no doubt in my mind that God had provided the opportunity I'd been given to fly to Indianapolis, Indiana, with a friend who was a physical therapist. We were to attend a workshop on lymphedema that was open only to doctors and physical therapists. I was neither.

But I suffered from this condition that caused tremendous swelling in my arm, a result of surgery for cancer. Because my physical therapist knew of the great interest I had in the subject, she arranged for me to attend with her. On top of that, every expense would be paid except my plane fare of $153.27.

I eagerly accepted her invitation and started asking God to help provide the money for me to go. I knew from the start it would take a miracle because our budget was stretched as tight as it could go toward medical bills we incurred while fighting the cancer. But it wasn't hard for me to believe in miracles—I was living proof!

God had chosen to heal me of cancer, yet this condition remained. I was sure there was a reason. Maybe he wanted to use me to help find a cure for this problem, which affects millions of people. Before me was a rare opportunity to research and learn more about the condition from a medical point of view.

I was to meet my friend in a half hour at the travel agency to pay for and pick up my plane ticket.

I glanced in my rearview mirror and saw a small black sports car back out and then pull back into its parking space. As I watched, it backed out again, and I recognized the driver. Beverly Easton was a lady from my luncheon group.

Was she having car trouble? She slowly drove out of the parking lot, circled the restaurant, and pulled back in again. This time she stopped in the middle of the lot, got out, and walked toward my car. I wondered if she thought I was the one having car trouble. Beverly stuck her head through my open passenger window.

"I know you don't know me very well, and I hope you don't think I'm crazy," she said. "I'm so embarrassed. Please don't be offended by this..."

My curiosity was stirred. "What's the matter, Beverly?"

"Well," she hesitated. "Several months ago God told me to put change in an envelope for you. I've just carried it around and have been adding to it every day till I got the nerve to give it to you. I hope this isn't insulting."

Her face flamed red as she tossed a bulging envelope onto the car seat.

"I just have to obey God," she mumbled, darting to her car before I could respond.

Makeup smudges and ink smears covered the once white envelope. On the front, my name was scribbled in big letters. Inside, a card explained that she wasn't sure why, but God had told her to give me this money. It was dated several months earlier. With tears in my eyes, I carefully emptied the contents out on the seat and started counting. There were bills of all denominations and lots of change.

The Bible says in Hebrews 13:8 that God is the same yesterday, today, and forever. If he provided his followers in Bible days with what they needed, he can and will do the same for his followers today. What an awesome God he is.

This time it wasn't a lake he used, but a lady named Beverly. And it wasn't a fish, but an envelope. One that contained *exactly* $153.27.

LOIS SPOON

The Day We Let Our Son Live

Approximately 90 percent of people who receive a prenatal diagnosis of Down syndrome decide to terminate their pregnancy.

A specialist had told us what no expecting parent wants to hear: "Something is very wrong with this baby."

Frightened and uncertain of our baby's future, we agreed to an amniocentesis. We would not, we thought, consider aborting our child, but we wanted to know what to expect. And this situation wasn't really covered in *What to Expect When You're Expecting*. Al held my hand while the doctor extracted amniotic fluid from my womb using a long needle. The doctor explained that it would take around two weeks to receive the results and mentioned when we would need to make a decision regarding termination.

Later that evening, after we'd both had some time to process the news, Al and I talked. I felt lost. This scenario didn't fit any of my plans. We talked about funerals and, if the baby survived, what life would be like for us and for him.

"What should we do?" I asked. "I never thought I would even think this, but do you think it would be more compassionate to terminate the pregnancy?" I felt horrible even thinking about abortion, but given what the doctor told us, I honestly wondered which was the more loving thing to do: to save him from the pain he would likely experience if he survived or to allow him to live.

After a moment of silence, Al responded, "I think we should do no harm." Relieved, I quietly agreed. From that moment on we began to prepare ourselves to welcome our son into this world regardless of what that looked like.

The most important day in my life is the day we decided to let our son live. We began to refer to him as Elijah instead of "the baby." We decided that even if he didn't survive the pregnancy, he was alive now, and we would enjoy him as long as we could.

A couple of weeks later, the doctor called with the results of the amniocentesis. Elijah was diagnosed with trisomy 21, more commonly known as Down syndrome, a condition caused by an extra twenty-first chromosome. We had done some research. We knew that a diagnosis of Down syndrome meant that Elijah would have difficulty learning. We knew he would experience developmental delays, such as walking and talking later than typical children. We also knew he was more likely to have a congenital heart defect and other medical problems.

The doctor asked if we had made a decision regarding termination. I was surprised. "Why would we terminate? It's only Down syndrome!" I was actually relieved. Elijah would most likely survive. I had no idea at the time how many parents in the same situation make the opposite choice.

Although we were glad Elijah would most likely live, we still grieved our lost hopes for a "perfect baby." I vacillated between mourning, "This is not what I planned for my life!" and making new plans. I spent many evenings crying—pregnancy hormones were bad enough, but a difficult diagnosis made things even worse. We read whatever books we could find about Down syndrome. We contacted the National Association for Down Syndrome and were paired with a support family. I was put on partial bed rest and spent a lot of time at the maternal health specialist's office for appointments and non-stress tests.

On April 8, 37 weeks into the pregnancy, I gave birth to Elijah Timothy Hsu, and after several difficult weeks, Elijah was released from the hospital.

Other than having Down syndrome, most of the other "abnormalities" the doctor listed were not present. Today Elijah is a happy and healthy four-year-old. He loves preschool and is learning to read. He communicates using a combination of sign language and spoken words. He enjoys giving hugs, dancing, and babbling in front of a mirror. His smile lights up a room, and his laugh is contagious. He and his seven-year-old brother, Josiah, play and fight together like any siblings. He often throws his food off the table when he's finished eating, and once he colored on our white furniture with a purple marker.

Elijah has developmental delays and sometimes takes longer to learn new skills than do most four-year-olds, but for the most part he's a normal kid doing normal kid stuff. Elijah's first year was sometimes difficult and overwhelming, but life with Elijah has settled into its own routine. Taking care of him is not all that different from taking care of our typical child. And loving Elijah comes just as naturally to me as loving Josiah.

I can't imagine life without Elijah anymore. He brings us so much joy. I'm so glad he's alive and that he's a part of our family. And I look forward to the day when Elijah can tell me about the most important day of his life.

Ellen Hsu

Rewards for Honesty

Sometimes the truth hurts—and sometimes it doesn't.

My son Jason's successes have come mainly in baseball. For a few years, whenever Jason took the field or the basketball court, he was the smallest player on either team. One summer, his lack of height was all the more noticeable because he was a seventh grader playing in a seventh/eighth-grade league.

A fire-armed pitcher—more than a foot taller than my four-foot-nine son—blazed a fastball right down the pike. I'm not sure Jason even saw the ball. Strike one. The second pitch scorched across the plate for a called strike two. The third pitch, unintentionally I'm sure, came right at Jason. He turned to avoid being hit and fell to the ground. His bat went flying. His helmet bounced off. The ball seemed to have skimmed his shoulder.

"Take your base," said the umpire.

Standing in the third-base coach's box, I was happy just seeing Jason alive, much less getting a free base. But now he was saying something to the umpire. What was going on?

"It didn't hit me," Jason said to the ump.

"Take your base, son," said the ump.

Our fans were most likely thinking the same thing I was thinking: Take your base, son. You've been wounded, soldier; your war's over. You're going home...

"But honest, it didn't hit me," Jason pleaded.

The umpire looked at Jason and out to the infield ump, who just shrugged.

"Okay," said the ump, "the count is one and two."

Should I intervene? Make him take his base? Jason was already digging in his cleats in the batter's box. I mentally shrugged and headed back to the coach's box.

The towering pitcher rocked and fired a bullet right down the middle —the kind of pitch that would likely send the kid to the dugout. Instead, Jason ripped the ball into left-center for a stand-up double. Our crowd roared. The manager of the team in the field was standing a few feet behind me. He had no idea that the kid on second base was my son. He spit out his sunflower seed shells and slowly shook his head.

"Man," he said, "you gotta love that."

BOB WELCH

Taskmaster

Is doing it all, all at the same time, really the best way?

Busy moms do it out of necessity. Drivers do it at 60 mph. And teenagers do it better than anybody.

Multitasking. Once merely computer lingo, the word now describes life as we know it. Noshing on a burger while steering a car through traffic while fumbling with directions.

Gone are the days of one task at a time. Now we do everything simultaneously. Work. Play. Eat. Travel. We feel so efficient, so on top of things. Look, Ma—no hands!

But when one of those multiple tasks includes a human being, we may be missing what matters most: an eye-to-eye and heart-to-heart connection.

I watched a young mother at the post office sort through her mail, talk on her cell phone, and try to keep tabs on her toddler. Nothing too dangerous there. Except she tossed out a letter, only to realize she meant to keep it, called out to her wayward little girl without really getting her attention, and apologized numerous times into her phone, "Sorry…what did you say?"

The child was clearly frustrated. No doubt the caller on the other end of the line was too. Both of them received the same unintentional message: "You're third on my list of priorities right now."

Do we really have to do three things at once to feel productive?

Apparently we do, and I'm the worst of sinners.

While on the phone with a long-winded friend, I open my e-mail, turning down the computer speakers so she won't hear the telltale sound effects, even as I wave a sheet of fast-food coupons at my husband, pointing to what I want for lunch.

Or I'll take a stack of correspondence into our family room and tune in a movie I've been eager to see. Distracted by the film, I have to read each letter twice, neither really connecting with the dear person who's written to me nor fully getting involved with the story on the screen. When a family member joins me and starts to chat, I catch myself scribbling words that make little sense, trying to follow the movie out of the corner of my eye and only half-listening, half-nodding to whatever my loved one is saying.

Is there any hope for a multitasking mama?

Yup. A simple one: Follow the Lord's example.

When Jesus spoke with people, they had his complete attention. The Bible does not say, "And while he sanded wood and kept watch on a pot of stew, Jesus said…" He simply listened and then responded. Individually and compassionately.

In Jesus's meeting with the woman at the well—his longest one-on-one conversation recorded in Scripture—she was amazed that a Jew was even willing to speak to a Samaritan: "How can you ask me for a drink?" (John 4:9). The disciples were taken aback as well: They "returned and were surprised to find him talking with a woman" (verse 27).

Clearly Jesus put conversations first on his to-do list, ignoring what was politically correct or productively expedient. Nothing mattered more than this thirsty woman.

His disciples got the message: "No one asked, 'What do you want?' or 'Why are you talking with her?'" (verse 27).

She got the message too, putting aside her task in favor of talking to people: "Leaving her water jar, the woman went back to the town" (verse 28).

Now it's our turn to get the message: Relationships aren't a task. Listening intently is the most valuable gift we can give. And looking into the eyes of someone we care about is time wisely spent.

My New Year's resolution? Do one task at a time and do it well, always putting people first.

Sure, it's old school. About 2000 years old. Thank the Lord it's never too late to learn.

LIZ CURTIS HIGGS

No Dad to Call

What can Father's Day mean to the daughter of a single mom?

My youth group was hundreds of miles from home on a mission trip in New Orleans. We were piled in the van on the way back to the motel when someone yelled out, "I get the pay phone first!"

"Why?" another kid asked. "Who do you need to call?"

"It's Father's Day, dork!" came the reply.

Father's Day. I hadn't thought about that in years. As everyone scrambled for coins and planned out a calling schedule, I stared blankly out the window of the van.

My dad had died from a heart attack when I was four, and I remembered so little about him. As for Father's Day, it was a holiday I had pretty much pushed out of my mind—until today.

Back at the motel, I wandered around by myself while everyone else scurried for the phones. I felt so sad and so alone. Sure, I had my mom and my three brothers. But who was I supposed to call today? As the day went on, my sorrow turned into anger. Why did I have to be left out of today's celebration? Why couldn't God have taken someone else, some bad parent? My dad was a good guy. He loved his wife and kids. And just before he died, he had committed his life to Christ. He could have been doing great things for God if he hadn't been taken away. Away from me.

I thought about all the things I'd missed. I never had a dad to cheer for me at softball games. I had to find a substitute for father-daughter events. By the time the sun set on that Father's Day, I was convinced I had been wronged in a horrible, unforgivable way.

In the days that followed, we spent our mornings putting on a Bible school for the local kids. Then in the afternoon, we volunteered at a youth center. I was still feeling sad and angry, but I kept my feelings to myself, convinced no one would understand anyway.

Working with the little kids during the day wasn't so bad. In fact, sometimes it was a lot of fun. But at our nightly Bible study, I tuned out. As my friends shared special moments of each day and lessons God had taught them, I crossed my arms and mentally blocked out their voices. I wasn't in the mood for happy God-talk. I just wanted this mission trip to be over.

And it almost was. With just a few days left, I found myself at the youth center, helping six-year-old Devin with his craft for the day. By that time we all had our favorite kids. Devin was mine. He had been given a few cruel nicknames by the other kids at the center—"Devin Devil" was the most popular—and it wasn't hard to understand why. He was loud, defiant, and angry. He wore a constant frown. I loved trying to make him laugh, and every once in a while he'd drop the tough guy act just long enough for me to see there was a pretty sweet kid in there somewhere.

"Not quite so much glue," I advised as Devin squeezed what seemed to be half the bottle onto his construction paper. He scowled at me but put the bottle down. He picked through the pieces of colored tissue paper that were piled in the middle of the table. "Are you gonna be here for a long time, Heather?" he asked suddenly. His words and face were emotionless—he was playing it cool.

"Not really. Just for a few more days," I told him.

"Oh." For a second, he actually looked disappointed. "What do you have to leave for, anyway?"

"I don't live here. I live in Alabama. I have to go home."

"I don't ever want to go home," Devin declared fiercely.

"Why not?"

He picked up a piece of tissue and smooshed it down. "Because no one there loves me." His voice had lost all emotion again.

That was not the answer I was expecting. And I was shocked at the way he said it—as if it was no big deal.

"Devin, that's not true."

"Is too."

I started to argue but stopped, remembering what David, the youth center director, had told us. These kids did not lead easy lives. Most were from broken homes. Some were being raised by grandparents because their parents were in jail or had abandoned them. A lot of them saw drug use every day. Who was I to tell Devin that everything was really just fine at his house?

"There are lots of people here who love you," I finally said. "And God loves you an awful lot too."

He shrugged. He stuck a few more pieces of tissue paper down and then held up his creation. "Look—I made a stained glass window." He grinned from ear to ear. I'd never seen him do that.

"Great job, Dev."

He grabbed a marker, and I watched as he carefully wrote his name across the top of his paper, his knuckles turning white from the effort. And suddenly, I felt terribly ashamed. I had spent so much time that week pouting about what I didn't have that I'd completely forgotten about all the really good things in my life. I was going home to a house full of people who loved me. So maybe one of them wasn't my dad— still, right then, my family was looking pretty great.

A couple days later I said goodbye to Devin. He gave me a big hug and looked a little sad, but he said he'd only "probably" miss me.

It's been a few years since then, and I still think about Devin. I pray that someday he'll feel secure in someone's love.

I still think about my dad too, and sometimes it makes me sad to think of all I've missed. But when those moods come, I try to remember Devin and his difficult life. No matter how much I may think I'm missing, there's surely someone out there who would consider me very blessed.

HEATHER BERMINGHAM

A Child Is a Bargain at Any Price

The cost may be high, but the benefits are incalculable.

The government once calculated the cost of raising a child from birth to 18 and came up with $160,140 for a middle-income family. For those with kids, that figure might lead to wild fantasies: "Think of all the money we could have banked if not for [insert your child's name here]." For others, that number might confirm the decision to remain childless.

But $160,140 isn't so bad if you break it down. It translates into $8,896.66 a year, $741.38 a month, or $171.09 a week. That's a mere $24.37 a day! Just over a dollar an hour.

Still, you might think the best financial advice is not to have children if you want to be rich. In fact, it's just the opposite. What do you get for your $160,140? Naming rights—first, middle, and last! Glimpses of God every day. Giggles under the covers every night. More love than your heart can hold. Eskimo kisses and Velcro hugs. Endless wonder over rocks, ants, clouds, and warm cookies. A hand to hold, usually covered with jam. A partner for blowing bubbles, flying kites, building sandcastles, and skipping down the sidewalk in the pouring rain. Someone to laugh yourself silly with regardless of what the boss said or how your stocks performed that day.

For just $160,140, you never have to grow up. You get to finger paint, carve pumpkins, play hide-and-seek, catch lightning bugs, and never stop believing in Santa Claus. You have an excuse to keep reading the adventures of Piglet and Pooh, watching Saturday morning cartoons, going to Disney movies, and wishing on stars. You get to frame rainbows, hearts, and flowers under refrigerator magnets and collect spray-painted noodle wreaths for Christmas, handprints set in clay for Mother's Day, and cards with backward letters for Father's Day.

For $160,140, there is no greater bang for your buck. You get to be a hero just for retrieving a Frisbee off the garage roof, taking the training wheels off the bike, removing a splinter, filling the wading pool, coaxing a wad of gum out of bangs, or coaching a baseball team that never wins but always gets treated to pizza regardless. You get a front-row seat to history to witness the first step, first word, first bra, first date, and first time behind the wheel. You get education in psychology, nursing, criminal justice, communications, and human sexuality that no college can match.

In the eyes of children, you have all the power to heal a boo-boo, scare away the monsters under the bed, patch a broken heart, police a slumber party, ground them forever, and love them without limits, so one day they, like you, will love without counting the cost.

ANONYMOUS

One of Us

We can find meaning in our sorrows by reaching out to others.

I hated everything about my life.

I had spent 23 years in a loveless marriage with little respect, and now my divorce was final. I had to leave my dream house in Anderson, South Carolina, and move to a dilapidated rental on a dead-end street. Even worse, I matched that awful house. Staring at the dingy floor, I felt ugly, used up, and broken. So many years of my life gone. Wasted.

Dropping to my knees, I traced a huge split in the linoleum as I prayed, "God, help me. If you get me out of this, I'm yours. Whatever you want. I just need three things—to find a job, to start a new life, and to be loved."

With no college degree and little employment history, my options were limited. Then word of a job opportunity came through my previous mission work. I'd be managing My Sister's Place, a shelter in northern Georgia for homeless women and their children. The position would provide a place for me to live and a salary. I didn't think I had much left to offer, but at least I'd be needed and loved. It sounded too good to be true.

My Sister's Place took in addicts, alcoholics, singles, divorcées, women with children, and some who never learned to manage money.

I didn't demand perfection, but somehow after I arrived, housekeeping dropped off. Chores were forgotten and duties half done. After a month I awoke to discover dirty dishes in the sink, ants crawling over the countertop, beds unmade, and cups covering the coffee table. *God, you tricked me—you put me in charge of a bunch of women who act like spoiled teenagers.*

"None of you appreciate me!" I slapped the dirty counter. "Can't you see how hard I'm trying?" My hands shook as I slung the Tupperware cups into the sink. "When are you going to grow up? I don't like being here, in case you didn't notice. If any of you don't want to help out, you know where the door is."

They scattered like rats—all except Gail. I stomped back to the bedrooms and ordered the rest of them to get busy making beds. That night for supper, I fixed turkey again from our collection. A church had donated twelve.

After supper we went through our usual routine—family time, devotional, and prayer circle. I offered no prayers. I didn't even hold hands.

After we finished, I peeled off down the street in my van, screaming out to God. "This is too hard. I can't do it." I found a used fast-food napkin under the seat to wipe my eyes. "I still hate my life," I sobbed. "I'm lonely no matter how many women you stick me with." God seemed far away and silent.

I drove until almost midnight and then U-turned my car back toward home. Stepping out into the dewy air, I stood in the damp, overgrown grass in the front yard and listened to laughter. I realized the ruckus was coming from behind the house. My tennis shoes squished as I trudged toward the voices. Peeking around the corner, I spotted the women. In the darkness their lighted cigarettes dotted the back porch like tiny red beacons. I inhaled, recalling the days when I'd smoked. Way back when.

"That Ms. Carol, something riled her today."

"Yeah, I ain't getting in her way."

Then Gail piped up. "Y'all give her a break. She's one of us." She paused to take a drag from her cigarette. "She's got nowhere to go. We're her family now. We should treat her that way."

I didn't speak to any of them that night. I knew it was impossible—I could never be like them.

Early the next morning, I heard a faint knock on my bedroom door. Gail tiptoed in with a cup of coffee. "Here, Ms. Carol. Just the way you like it." She grinned and stuck her stubby hair behind her ears. "Sorry about yesterday. We're gonna do better."

"How come you smile all the time?" I grabbed the mug and moved over to give her room on my bed. Gail spent half her day in addiction classes and then went straight to Krystal's to flip burgers.

"I have so much," she said.

"Honey, look around. You don't have that much." I patted her skinny, tattooed arm.

"I have you," she said in her throaty voice. "I'm glad you're here. We need you. Bad." Smile lines formed at the edges of her 47-year-old blue eyes. Lines just like mine. Gail hugged me with all her might. In her arms, something angry inside me began to melt.

My sweet Lord, I thought. *I understand way too much about abusive relationships. You've been preparing me for this job for years. I know how they feel. I've been there…I am one of them.*

Later that day, I drove to the co-op to pick up free food. As I shopped I prayed, *God, show me how to really love these women.*

Filling up my bag with fruits and vegetables, I noticed something I'd never seen. Long-stem pink roses. They reminded me of my yard in South Carolina. The man behind the table said, "Take some. Every day, if you want. They'll just get thrown out."

Free roses! What woman doesn't love roses?

That night, we celebrated with store-bought hamburger meat—a rare treat. I took my time and made homemade spaghetti, and I found a vase under the sink for the pink roses. Smiling, I arranged donated candles all over the table. It looked special, like something I'd love myself.

"Attention, ladies," I said, tapping my tea glass with my fork. "We have a new tradition—our family's tradition. Every night we'll have fresh roses and candles on our table."

In the soft glow of candlelight, my precious family and I reached out and held hands as we said our blessing. Gail, my new sister and best friend, sat on my right side and squeezed my hand tightly. I squeezed back—hard.

CAROL HEATH

The Writing on the Wall

Can we hear the message even if we can't relate to the messenger?

Early in my ministry, I served a little church in rural Georgia. One Saturday we went to a funeral in a little country church not of my denomination. I grew up in a big downtown church. I had never been to a funeral like this one. The casket was open, and the funeral consisted of a sermon by the preacher.

The preacher pounded on the pulpit and looked over at the casket. He said, "It's too late for Joe. He might have wanted to get his life together. He might have wanted to spend more time with his family. He might have wanted to do that, but he's dead now. It is too late for him, but it's not too late for you. There is still time for you. You still can decide. You are still alive. It is not too late for you. Today is the day of decision."

Then the preacher told how a Greyhound bus had run into a funeral procession once on the way to the cemetery, and he warned that the same thing could happen today. He said, "You should decide today. Today is the day to get your life together. It's too late for old Joe, but it's not too late for you."

I was so angry at that preacher. On the way home, I told my wife, "Have you ever seen anything so manipulative and so insensitive to that poor family? I found it disgusting."

She said, "I've never heard anything like that. It was manipulative. It was disgusting. It was insensitive. Worst of all, it was also true."

WILL WILLIMON

Blind to Blessing

Sometimes God answers prayers in ways we don't expect.

My husband and I were about to start our graduate degree programs, hoping to squeak through school together living on love and Taco Bell. Charlie had a decent laptop, but my only computer was a three-inch-thick 1996 laptop. So for my birthday that July, I decided to ask our families for money for a new laptop. They were quite generous, and I received $720—enough to buy a nice new computer.

Before I made my purchase, we took a road trip to visit several college friends. Our old Nissan pickup—our only vehicle—had broken down shortly before our trip, so we left the truck at the shop and drove a borrowed car. During our trip our mechanic called with an estimate for repairs. It was more than we had expected, and we didn't know where we would get the money. I was so fixated on getting my new laptop, it didn't even occur to me to use the money I'd received for my birthday to fix the truck.

I told a friend when we were out for coffee about my plans to buy a laptop. She had recently gotten a new computer and offered me her old laptop. I still didn't take the hint. I thanked her but dismissed her offer. Her laptop, while several years newer than mine and certainly adequate for me to write papers on, was not the shiny new computer I'd set my sights on.

Back at the house where we were staying that night, Charlie and I were trying to figure out how we could scrape some money together to fix the truck. Somehow I finally allowed the thought I'd subconsciously been fighting off to enter my head: I could accept my friend's old computer and use my birthday money to fix our truck. I knew the Holy

Spirit was telling me to surrender my plans, and I knew that insisting on my own way would be saying no to him. So I yielded to the Spirit's prompting. As soon as I did, scales seemed to fall off the eyes of my heart as I suddenly remembered the number I had jotted down from the mechanic: $720. God knew I needed a computer. He also knew we needed a repaired truck. He provided a free computer, and he gave us the exact amount of money—to the dollar—that we needed to fix our truck.

We wrote that story down in a notebook we kept at the time, but not just to remind us of God's supernatural provision. As much as I rejoiced in God's provision, I was sobered by how blind I was for so long when it was right in front of my face. God wanted to bless me. He provided just what I needed in ways I couldn't have anticipated, but my greed almost kept me from receiving that blessing. What a warning to fix my gaze not on what my sinful heart lusts after but on my Father, who withholds no good thing from his children.

ALISON RITCH

The Nightly Ritual

We're never too old to have fun or to say "I love you."

When my sons were little, we used to join hands and have prayer at the end of the day. Then I'd give them a kiss goodnight. When my son Phil was about nine, he got in bed one night and said, "Mom, I can't remember whether Dad kissed me goodnight or not." So Judy told me. I tiptoed up the steps, bolted through his door like a monster, dove in his bed, and wrestled with him and tickled him. We laughed, and I kissed him. Then we just laid there in the darkness for about 15 minutes and talked—a rare and special time.

The next night he got in bed and said, "Mom, I can't remember whether Dad kissed me goodnight or not." So again I bounded through his door and jumped in his bed and wrestled and tickled and laughed.

Every night for weeks after that, as soon as we said "Amen," he would run away from me and get in bed and say, "Dad, you didn't kiss me goodnight." I would then have to come and jump in his bed and wrestle and carry on. It was a great ritual.

One night we were wrestling and carrying on in his room. I finally said goodnight and walked past his older brother's room. "Goodnight, Russ," I said. He said, "Goodnight, Dad." I got to thinking, *Every night Russ hears us laughing and carrying on in the next room. Then I go by and just say goodnight. Maybe he'd want me to do that to him.* So I bolted through his room, jumped in his bed, and started wrestling with him— nearly got whipped, if I remember! It settled down, and I decided it was time for me to express how I felt. I have to be honest: I sometimes have a hard time saying to a person what I want to say. I said, "Rusty, I want you to know how proud I am of you and how special I think you are.

I want you to know I love you." He said, "Okay, Dad." No big thing! But I felt better because I had expressed it.

The next morning, as I was walking by his door, Russ said, "Dad, could you come in here a minute?" I went in. He hemmed and hawed a bit and pawed the floor, and said, "Dad, thank you for coming in last night. I never get too old for that."

BOB RUSSELL

Jesus Is Missing!

Or maybe he's hidden in plain sight.

The boxes of Christmas decorations were carried up from the basement.

I had to go to church, so the serious work of decorating our home would have to wait until I returned. In the meantime, our five-year-old daughter, Lauren, was content to play with a miniature plastic nativity set we keep in an old Life Savers tin. When I arrived home, I was greeted by my wife, Wendy, and the inviting aroma of dinner. Stealing a peek at the table, I saw that Lauren had placed pieces of the nativity set at each person's plate. Apparently shepherds, wise men, cows, and sheep would be joining us for dinner. Very sweet.

Just then Lauren raced into the kitchen. "Oh, Daddy, Daddy!" Her voice was panicked. "Jesus is missing! We've looked everywhere and can't find him!" She was right. As I glanced at the supper table, I didn't see baby Jesus anywhere. "We'll find him," I said, sure that he was stuck under the couch cushions or behind a chair somewhere. "Let's look after we eat."

And look we did—high and low. Under the couch, in the plants, in the Barbie playhouse...We scoured Lauren's coloring desk and found stickers, markers, crayons, and a half-full can of pop—everything but Jesus! As my compulsive "find whatever is lost at any cost" neurosis kicked into high gear, I zeroed in on Lauren's backpack.

Much like her older sisters, Lauren carries her backpack everywhere she goes. In it she transports her treasures: hairbows, hats, Barbies, her stuffed kitty, Polly Pockets, a plastic wallet, Gummi Bears...and sure enough, there at the bottom of her treasure trove was Jesus. "Here he is!" I proudly announced. "Jesus was in your backpack, ready to go with you to preschool tomorrow."

I've often reflected on the search for our MIA Jesus, and I now realize that he wasn't missing in action at all. He was in the middle of the action. His place in Lauren's backpack was divinely appropriate. There, in the midst of all the symbols of my daughter's interests and activities, was the Lord of life.

As we face a schedule crammed with commitments, each of us can be confident that Jesus is right there in the middle of it all. As much as it drives us crazy not to have the Jesus piece in its proper place in the crèche (or at the dinner table), he belongs in our minivans, briefcases, purses, gym bags, suitcases, and checkbooks. God's uncontainable love for his creation spilled over into a manger, a carpenter's shop, a fishing boat, a tax collector's home, a Roman execution scene, a rich man's grave, and an upper room. The good news of Christmas that catapults us toward Easter and beyond is that we are not alone. The one who made us has come to us and remains with us in all that we attempt.

GREG ASIMAKOUPOULOS

The (Not So) Terrible Year

How can trials possibly be our friends?

I'm sitting in yet another hospital waiting room.

Since my husband, Barry, first underwent open heart and quadruple bypass surgery 15 months ago, I've been in this waiting room—or one just like it—more times than I can count on one hand, waiting for him to come out of the operating room.

In little more than a year's time, my vocabulary has increased to include words and phrases such as *aneurysm, atrial fib,* and *EP study with ablation.* They all mean I have to put on a cheery face, kiss Barry goodbye, and promise I won't worry about him or forget to eat lunch and lock the garage door at night while he's in the hospital again.

With all Barry's surgeries and procedures, we've had a terrible, horrible, no good, very bad year—one of the worst in our 32 years together. Yet ironically, it's also turned out to be the best.

I learned just how deeply Barry loves me. As he was all prepped and waiting to go into surgery to repair his aortic aneurysm, Barry looked at my friend Tara, who was waiting with us, and said, "Make sure Nancy takes care of herself. Promise me, or else I'll worry."

He wasn't worried about being sliced open again—he was worried about me.

I came to faith in Christ three years after Barry and I married, and for almost 30 years I prayed about my husband's relationship with the Lord. Then the day of Barry's open-heart surgery, he told me if he died, I'd see him again, because he knew Jesus was his Savior. He prayed with me, he prayed with a friend, and he prayed with his surgeon. Barry hasn't stopped praying—he prays with me every day.

What I'd asked God for all these years—to heal the spiritual rift in my marriage, to bring my husband and me close—God had given. He'd performed heart surgery on us both, ripping us apart and knitting us back together.

Barry and I talk often about this past year, how it's been awful—and awfully good. We wouldn't wish this kind of year on anyone and wouldn't want to go through it again, but we're glad it happened.

We thank God for the good days and the bad because in all our days God has held us both securely in his grip. We've known God's incredible kindness to us. Our hearts are in his hands.

We've had a terrible, horrible, no good, very bad year—and I praise God for it.

NANCY KENNEDY

Daddy's Baby Has Come Home

But is Daddy ready for what he'll see?

On a short flight from Tucson to Phoenix, I noticed a young woman with her baby. They were both dressed in white pinafores. The mother was smiling, and the little baby was saying "Dada, Dada." And the little baby was darling. She wore a little pink bow where there would probably be hair pretty soon, and it was just darling. And they sat down opposite me. Every time anybody went by, the baby would say, "Dada, Dada."

The young mother said they were going home, and Daddy was waiting for them. I think they had been gone overnight—it was a long, long time like that!

Everybody was so happy, and we all enjoyed the little baby. The mother had a little thermos with orange juice in it. She kept feeding the baby, a little fruit and then a little juice. It was a rough flight. Every time the baby cried the mother fed her a little bit more orange juice and a little more fruit.

I don't know how to get out of this story without telling you the truth. The flight was so turbulent that the attendants had to stay seated. All of the fruit that had gone down came up. I think more came up than had gone down; I think there was more up than there was baby, and it was startling. The carpet was not in good condition. It was a mess.

Those of us on the opposite side of the aisle were not in good condition at all. We kept trying to tell the young mother it was just fine. We were handing her tissues and things. (Most of us have been babies.) It was a very loving time, but a mess. The baby was crying, and she looked awful. We couldn't cry, but we looked awful. The mother was so sorry about it.

We landed. The minute we landed, baby was fine: "Dada, Dada." The rest of us were just awful. We began to get off the plane, and we all moved very carefully. I had on a suit, and I was trying to decide whether to burn it or just cut off the sleeve. Have you ever tried to get away from something really unpleasant and it was you? Well, that's the way we were. It was really bad.

I looked out of the plane, and there waiting was the young man who had to be Daddy: white slacks, white shirt, white flowers, and a little green paper. I thought, *I know what's going to happen. He's going to run to that baby who now looks awful*—I mean the hair and the pinafore were dreadful—*he's going to run to that baby, get one look, and keep on running, saying, "Not my kid!"*

As he ran to the young mother, I wouldn't say she threw the baby at him, but she did kind of leave quickly to go get cleaned up. I watched as he picked up that baby and hugged her and kissed her and stroked her hair. He said, "Daddy's baby has come home. Daddy's baby has come home."

I watched them all the way to the luggage claim area. He never stopped kissing that baby. He never stopped welcoming that baby back home. I thought, *Where did I ever get the idea that my Father God is less loving than a young daddy in white slacks and white shirt with white flowers and a green paper?*

JEANNETTE CLIFT GEORGE

Living with an Intruder

For some of us, there's only one way to learn about
love and service in the name of Christ.

The intruder invaded Elizabeth's body, and by extension, mine. Her disease became my disease and made relational demands we were ill-prepared to manage. As she moved from cane to walker to electric scooter and finally to a powered wheelchair, and then as she lost the use of her right hand, I had to adjust my life to fit her needs.

Uninvited and unwelcome, this disease now forces us into a kind of sick reality game, leaving no choice but to follow the rules even as they change and become more restrictive.

Every family divvies up chores, fairly or not so fairly. The multiple sclerosis dictates ours, and it's not at all fair, but we do have the choice to let it tear us apart or use it to strengthen our marriage bond as we face the adversity together. This reaches deeper than deciding who does what. It reaches to feelings, emotions, and attitudes about what we do, what's done to us, and who we are to ourselves and each other.

We both pray for healing. With our families and our church, we agonize before God for a return to the day when Elizabeth can offer an open handshake instead of a permanently clenched fist or take a flight of stairs without thought.

But if we only grieve the loss, we miss the gain—that what this disease does to us may also be done for us. Even as the MS steals abilities from Elizabeth's life, a healing grows almost undetected inside. When we talk about this, Elizabeth wonders aloud, "Did it really take this to teach me that my soul is more important to God than my body?"

And I ask, "Is this what Jesus meant when he taught his disciples to serve? When he washed their feet, did he look 2000 years into the future and see me washing my wife's clothes and helping her onto her shower seat to bathe? Did it really take this to teach me compassion?"

God's healing can be sneaky. We pray that Elizabeth will resume her old life; he wants her to assume a new life. We long for change on the outside; he desires change on the inside. We pray for what we want; he answers with what he knows we need.

God has made me question whom I love. When I pray for healing, is it for Elizabeth's sake? Or is it because her healing would make life so much easier for me? I challenge, "Aren't you the God who heals? I love her and I want her well." But in the back of my mind I know I also want her healed for my benefit.

In response to my challenge, Jesus asks me as he asked Peter, "Do you love me more than these?" I think, *He wants me to love him more than I love my wife.* So I reply with Peter's words, "Yes, Lord. You know that I love you."

"Tend my lambs," he tells me.

The exposure shames me. Do I love him more than these? This is the love of Matthew 22:37-39, which commands me to love God with all that's within me, with all my heart, soul, and mind, and to love my neighbor—my wife—as I would myself.

Loving what I want for myself isn't even on Jesus's list. It's not in me to love the way he tells me to, but God has promised that his love "has been poured out into our hearts through the Holy Spirit, who has been given to us" (Romans 5:5). God has given me an impossible command, but he has given me the power to obey it.

The intruder still resides in our home, still presents us with new challenges each day, and still teaches us forceful lessons on submission, dependence, service, and a love that endures all things and never fails—even when I fail.

Strange as it may seem, that intruder is beginning to look more and more like a guest.

DICK PETERSON

Flying Lesson

A young traveling companion helped me with my baggage.

The two-hour flight to Dallas was minutes from takeoff as I settled into aisle seat 7B and began to pray for whoever might sit in 7A.

Not for his or her soul, though that would have been the right and holy thing to do. No, I was praying about this person's size. Hoping the stranger would be petite and/or patient, someone who wouldn't feel miserable squished next to an abundantly blessed woman. In a roomy 737, no problem; in a tiny commuter plane with every seat sold, big problem. *Please, Lord. Someone kind. And small.*

As I watched the passengers file past, I mentally rehearsed my opening patter: *They keep making these planes smaller, don't they?* Or *Sure wish my hips could fit in the overhead compartment!* Anything to put him or her at ease and avoid an embarrassing scene. Moments later, a slender, smiling boy appeared by my seat. "I'm 7A."

"So you are!" I crowed. *Thank you, Lord.* He had blond hair, round eyeglasses, and the pink cheeks of late childhood. I pegged him at nine or ten, maybe even a mature eight.

He climbed into his seat, barely taking up half of it, and announced, "I like this plane. It's my size." He leaned toward me and added in a stage whisper, "It makes me feel bigger."

Bless his heart. I asked his name, wondering what it must be like to travel alone at such a young age, and then gently patted his arm. "I'm here if you need anything."

After he drifted off to sleep, I resisted the maternal urge to smooth back the hair that fell across his brow. *So young, so vulnerable.*

When the engines grew louder, signaling our descent, my young neighbor woke with a yawn, glanced at his watch, and grinned. "Whadya know? My birthday's next week."

I beamed at him, picturing the big party his parents would throw. "A birthday, is it?"

"Yeah. I'll be 15."

My smile froze in place. *It couldn't be!* Not this small boy, no taller than a third grader.

Think of the snide comments his peers must throw at him! Not to mention the many clueless strangers—such as me—who treat him as though he's a half-grown child instead of a full-fledged teenager.

"Happy birthday," I murmured, my heart breaking. What must it be like to be smaller than people expect?

The answer came from deep inside: *It's like being larger than people expect.*

Oh, Lord. Of course.

I looked down and fumbled with my seat belt, suddenly feeling exposed. Just as this self-conscious teen kept his defense tactics at the ready—"It's my size" and "My birthday's next week"—I had my verbal arsenal loaded as well, deflecting imagined criticism by beating people to the punch—*They keep making these planes smaller, don't they?*

No, Liz. They don't.

The time had come to see my self-effacing banter for what it was: fear of rejection.

You won't like me. You won't approve. You'll say something unkind.

The apostle Paul once asked, "Am I now trying to win the approval of human beings, or of God?" (Galatians 1:10). I was trying to please people, all right. Or spare myself their displeasure. God, sorry to say, hadn't entered into the equation at all.

I needed to pray, not for my own comfort, but for the opportunity to comfort another. To pray not to be loved, but for a chance to demonstrate Christ's love to a stranger. To be more other-conscious and less self-conscious. To seek God's approval *alone*.

Resolving to do better on the next leg of my trip, I looked up and caught the small teenager watching me with a curious gaze.

"You okay, ma'am?" he asked as the wheels touched the runway.

"More than okay." I grinned. "Thanks to you."

LIZ CURTIS HIGGS

Swords or Paintbrushes?

Is life a problem to be solved or a medium for creation?

My friend and I sat on my patio, drinking tea and catching up with life. She had just moved to a new situation, away from familiar work, beautiful spaces, and valued friends. Now she was experiencing the exhausting emptiness of a job that was too full, a context where she felt undervalued, and a place where friends were not naturally found. The tears filled her eyes as she spoke of her weariness, her disillusionment, and her anger. My friend is a fighter. She wants to right wrongs for herself and others; she wants to demand a human pace and human respect. She wants to know and be known. And she has been fighting hard for what she wants.

After the first cup of tea, I offered her this observation from Dorothy Sayers: "Life is not a problem to be solved, but a medium for creation." And I suggested, "Perhaps it's time to drop your sword and pick up your paintbrush."

And we were off, exploring the internal battles that we so often fight with others even when they never experience the swordplay in our souls.

We spoke of the weariness created by internal turmoil and that lack of quiet within ourselves that adds to the general frenetic emptiness. And then we turned to the palette of colors she had been given in this season—not the rich reds, golds, and blues that this friend would naturally reach for, but a more subdued set of tones: grays, browns, and maybe a few tans. Could there be beauty in this season? Could life be a medium for creation—even here?

It is not the first conversation I have had in the past week on the difference between a full life and a frenetic one. And I find myself increasingly recognizing that when there are so very few things over which we have control, we still have the choice of whether to wield a sword or pick up a paintbrush.

I have no idea what beauty the Lord will create through my friend in this season—how large or small a canvas she will be given or what colors may appear on her palette. But I do know this: In most seasons of life, beauty accomplishes a great deal more than anger, and a brush rests more easily in our hands than a sword. And so I hugged her good-bye with this prayer in my heart: "May the favor [or beauty] of the Lord our God rest on us; establish the work of our hands for us—yes, establish the work of our hands" (Psalm 90:17).

CARLA WATERMAN

Prayer from Far Away

*A minister shares a story of how God used his
youngest son to teach him a valuable lesson about
prayer and the nature of God's presence.*

One day I was leaving for work when my wife said she wasn't feeling well. After quizzing her for a moment to find out what was wrong, I decided I should take a personal day. But she insisted everything was fine and told me to go ahead with my plans.

As I was about to leave the house, I thought, *I should make sure our son knows how to call me in case of an emergency.* So I asked him to come to our bedroom, where I was making the bed. I sat him down and walked him through the simple process of calling my cell phone. To ensure he had retained the lesson and wouldn't have any trouble later on, I had him give it a try right there on the spot. I watched him dial my number from our home phone, my cell rang, I answered, and for just a minute or so, we had a nice, little conversation standing ten feet from each other in the same room.

After we wrapped up the conversation, my son left the room. *Okay,* I thought. *If there's a problem while I'm gone, the little man of the house can reach me.* About three minutes later, my cell vibrated again, and when I glanced to check who was calling, I saw my home phone number. Still standing in the bedroom, I answered the phone with a smile.

"Hello?"

"Hey, Dad," came the familiar voice. "I just wanted to call from the living room to make sure this phone works from far way!"

I chuckled and shared with my son that our house phone works very well. I told him that he could even call China from our phone if he wanted to—and then immediately made it clear that he shouldn't call China!

The moment has since served as a gentle reminder for me about a simple truth we find in Scripture. When I walk through a valley, I sometimes wonder if God hears me. I feel "far away" from him. The same fear is stirred when I stray from God. I'm afraid he can't hear me because I've drifted too far. But I know prayer works even from far away because God always has his eyes on me wherever I go. The psalmist puts it this way: "You know when I sit and when I rise; you perceive my thoughts from afar" (Psalm 139:2). It really doesn't matter where I go. Prayer works even from far away.

PETER CHARPENTIER

The Sparrow at Starbucks

One song silenced the cappuccino machine.

It was chilly in Manhattan but warm inside the Starbucks on Fifty-First Street and Broadway, just a skip up from Times Square. Early November weather in New York City holds only the slightest hint of the bitter chill of late December and January, but it's enough to send the masses crowding indoors to vie for available space and warmth.

For a musician, it's the most lucrative Starbucks location in the world, I'm told, and consequently, the tips can be substantial if you play your tunes right. Apparently, we were striking all the right chords that night, because our basket was almost overflowing.

It was a fun, low-pressure gig—I was playing keyboard and singing backup for my friend who also added rhythm with an arsenal of percussion instruments. We mostly did pop songs from the '40s to the '90s with a few original tunes thrown in. During our emotional rendition of the classic "If You Don't Know Me by Now," I noticed a lady sitting in one of the lounge chairs across from me. She was swaying to the beat and singing along.

After the tune was over, she approached me. "I apologize for singing along on that song. Did it bother you?" she asked.

"No," I replied. "We love it when the audience joins in. Would you like to sing up front on the next tune?"

To my delight, she accepted my invitation.

"You choose," I said. "What are you in the mood to sing?"

"Well...do you know any hymns?"

Hymns? This woman didn't know whom she was dealing with. I

cut my teeth on hymns. Before I was even born, I was going to church. I gave our guest singer a knowing look. "Name one."

"Oh, I don't know. There are so many good ones. You pick one."

"Okay," I replied. "How about 'His Eye Is on the Sparrow'?"

My new friend was silent, her eyes averted. Then she fixed her eyes on mine again and said, "Yeah. Let's do *that* one."

She slowly nodded her head, put down her purse, straightened her jacket, and faced the center of the shop. With my two-bar setup, she began to sing.

Why should I be discouraged?
Why should the shadows come?

The audience of coffee drinkers was transfixed. Even the gurgling noises of the cappuccino machine ceased as the employees stopped what they were doing to listen. The song rose to its conclusion.

I sing because I'm happy;
I sing because I'm free.
His eye is on the sparrow,
and I know he watches me.

When the last note was sung, the applause crescendoed to a deafening roar that would have rivaled a sold-out crowd at Carnegie Hall. Embarrassed, the woman tried to downplay the response.

But the ovation continued. I embraced my new friend. "You, my dear, have made my whole year! That was beautiful!"

"Well, it's funny that you picked that particular hymn," she said.

"Why is that?"

"Well..." she hesitated again, "that was my daughter's favorite song."

"Really!" I exclaimed.

"Yes," she said, and then grabbed my hands. By this time, the applause had subsided, and it was business as usual. "She was 16. She died of a brain tumor last week."

I said the first thing that found its way through my stunned silence. "Are you going to be okay?"

She smiled through tear-filled eyes and squeezed my hands. "I'm gonna be okay. I've got to keep trusting the Lord and singing his songs, and everything's gonna be just fine."

She picked up her bag and gave me her card, and then she was gone.

Was it just a coincidence that we happened to be singing in that particular coffee shop on that particular November night? Coincidence that this wonderful lady just happened to walk into that particular shop? Coincidence that of all the hymns to choose from, I just happened to pick the very hymn that was the favorite of her daughter, who had died just the week before? I refuse to believe it.

God has been arranging encounters in human history since the beginning of time, and it's no stretch for me to imagine that he could reach into a coffee shop in midtown Manhattan and turn an ordinary gig into a revival. It was a great reminder that if we keep trusting him and singing his songs, everything's gonna be okay.

JOHN THOMAS OAKS

Hiding What They Seek

*In my desire to be seeker friendly, I'm
often guilty of concealing Jesus.*

A friend was involved for years in a weekly service intended to reach out to inner-city kids, the majority of whom had little church experience and no acknowledged relationship with Jesus.

If it had been up to me, I would have made those events "seeker friendly." I'd have focused on building relationships, avoiding anything too religious or high pressure. But my friend went a different way. Every week, he led worship, one song after another, always unabashedly about—or to—Jesus.

I'm sure some of the kids walked away and never looked back. But hundreds stayed. Many made decisions to follow Christ.

Some ministry leaders were concerned that teens who didn't know Jesus were being asked to participate in worship. My friend would reply, "How else are they supposed to get to know him?"

It's a good question. People come to the Christian faith via many different highways, but the eventual crossroad is always an encounter with Jesus. I wonder if my attempts to keep my witness nonthreatening and accessible sometimes end up shielding the unchurched people around me from their own crossroad. Jesus can certainly meet them without my assistance. But I would rather be a help than a hindrance.

I was definitely a hindrance in Mexico. My husband, Mark, is a public high school counselor. A few years ago, a group of eleventh graders asked him to coordinate a humanitarian trip. He contacted one of our favorite Christian organizations, and they agreed to facilitate an excursion to Mexico to build a playground in an impoverished area. Mark was careful to explain that the students participating were unchurched; should there be even a whiff of proselytizing, parents and the school board would feel betrayed.

There were twenty-four students and four teachers; my kids and I tagged along. Upon arrival, we discovered that the arranged accommodations at a local Rotary Club house had fallen through. Instead, we would be sleeping on the cement floor of a church basement in downtown Juárez, one of the most dangerous cities in Mexico. Mark could already imagine the parent phone calls he'd receive when word trickled home. Weary from a long day of travel, we set up sleeping bags and tried to ignore the exposed wiring, hole-ridden walls, and scurry of cockroaches.

In the morning, we drove to the site of our project. Jaws dropped and eyes welled as we observed the abject poverty around us. But we also experienced the sweet rush of doing something worthwhile. At the end of the day, we returned to our cement floor feeling good.

All was well until the nausea hit. Sometime around three a.m., the first wave of students became ill; by morning, clusters of miserable people were draped on every available garbage can. Mark held his head and imagined a new wave of parent phone calls. Mostly he threw up.

Around nine a.m., the two local women who were preparing our food arrived on the scene and surveyed the carnage. Despite the language barrier, their distress and concern were unmistakable. They had followed all the guidelines for cooking for foreigners, and we were still sick. Eventually, one of the women approached the only teacher who could speak Spanish and asked for permission to pray for us. Too ill to object, the teacher nodded yes.

As soon as the woman began to pray, I knew we were in trouble. I thought, *Maybe everyone is so ill they won't mind the praying.* But my hopes for a low-impact prayer faded quickly as the woman became increasingly emotional. She prayed for five minutes. Ten. Maybe more.

Gracias Padre, Gracias Jesús, Gracias Espíritu Santo, she wept, over and over. I began a prayer of my own. *Please make her stop. I don't want Mark to get fired. I don't want these kids to be put off of religion.*

When she was finally done, I took a deep breath and forced myself to raise my flushed face, dreading the reactions I knew were inevitable.

Things were not as I expected.

There was not a dry eye in the room. Students were hushed, visibly moved. "That was beautiful," whispered one teacher. Several people nodded. To them, the prayer had been not unwelcome proselytizing, but a heart cry—passionate, desperate, and utterly authentic.

I was ashamed, of course, and humbled. The Holy Spirit had been moving, and I, one of the few mature believers in the room, had missed it.

I wish I had prayed different prayers in Mexico. These days, in increasing measure, I do. When faced with potential encounters with the living God, even among the uninitiated, I am learning to pray *Yes* and *Thank you* rather than *Stop*. After all, how else are any of us supposed to get to know him?

CAROLYN ARENDS

A Cast of Thousands

Efficiency doesn't always equal effectiveness.

At my daughter's elementary school musical, the printed program noted, "This musical was originally written for 15 actors, but it has been adapted to accommodate our cast of 206." You know what kind of show this was. No-cut auditions, no performer left without something special to do. They danced, they sang, they delivered lines, and somehow 206 children graced the stage that night.

It was not a short program.

Church leaders are like the volunteer geniuses who took a musical with parts for 15 and creatively made room for 206. We could professionalize our task and simply pay someone to do it, but we divide it into parts so that everyone has a job. Is it efficient? No, not if all we cared about was getting the job done. But the church cares less about getting the job done and more about the people doing it. We are not in the efficiency business. Our business is to make disciples. We want to offer as many people as possible the chance to know Christ in service and in community.

I have sat in church meetings where the most unlikely person volunteered for a job. The woman I had envisioned on the finance committee chooses instead to join a team of church supper cooks. We want her excellent mind and keen eye keeping track of our numbers, but that's what she does all day.

"At church, I want to do what I love," she says, and until then, I never knew that she loved cooking. That church supper could have been catered with more efficiency, but instead the script was adapted to accommodate a person with a calling.

Sure, there are people we might not want on the program. Sometimes the accountant reminds us how grateful we are that cooking is not her day job. We have to adjust, to help her find the place where her gifts meet the world's needs. But as we bite into a half-cooked quiche or rubbery sausage, we remember that Jesus's call extends to all of us, not just the star performers or even the competent.

The church remains the home of the no-cut audition. We don't get to choose the other members of our body. You have to want to get in, but once you are here, we will find a part for you to play.

LILLIAN DANIEL

A Purpose-Driving Life

*I wanted to do great and grand things. I
ended up hauling girls everywhere.*

Years ago someone asked me what I wanted on my tombstone. I
replied, rather flippantly, "She drove girls."

At the time I had a red '89 Ford Tempo with 189,000 miles on it,
and I was sure I had driven 188,000 of those miles hauling girls to the
mall and volleyball practice, to softball games and the mall, to the mall
and the church youth group, to the beach, to Taco Bell, to school, to
the mall…

I could either drive them or risk them finding rides with someone's
sister's boyfriend. As long as my daughters and their myriad of clos-
est friends were in the backseat of my car with me at the wheel, I knew
where they were. It may be a control thing, but it's a common sense
thing too. I didn't realize it at the time, but it was also a ministry thing.

Not too long ago, Kelly's mother called to thank me for what I'd
done for her daughter. Kelly, who had died of leukemia at age 21, had
been my daughter Laura's best childhood friend.

At first I thought she was thanking me for reading something I'd
written for Kelly's funeral, but I realize now she meant something else,
which brings me back to my purpose-driving life.

Years before, I'd prayed that God would give me a grand purpose
in life. He answered by giving me two daughters and a set of car keys.

"Drive," he said.

So drive I did—and became known among the other moms as
Transportation Central. And I loved every minute of it.

It actually proved to be quite educational. I learned I could be invisible. The girls would all pile into my car and start talking about the stuff girls talk about—mostly boys and other girls. They would start dishing the dirt as if I weren't even in the car.

You can learn a lot by being invisible, and as I listened to their conversations and drove, you can bet I also prayed!

During my years of driving girls, my car was used as a cafeteria, a beauty parlor, a dressing room, a last-minute study hall, a laundry hamper, and a place to take a nap.

It was also at times a confessional and a sanctuary. Something amazing happened when my little red Tempo filled with girls.

God got in too.

Sometimes I wonder if those girls in the backseat realized his presence. I think maybe they did, because every once in a while (when they acknowledged my presence) they asked me questions about my Christian faith or my opinion of Ouija boards or levitating. We discussed Buddhism, paganism, and Marilyn Manson. Sometimes I even prayed out loud for them.

It was all so very natural, yet not. It was mundane and ordinary, yet incredibly holy. Now that my daughters are grown, I actually miss those days.

At one time I'd wanted to be somebody important, to do great and grand things. I ended up driving girls. It wasn't what I'd envisioned, but for a good portion of my life it was what I'd been created and called to do.

Jesus told his followers that God cares about sparrows. He commended a poor widow who gave two meager pennies, affirmed faith the size of a mustard seed, and likened the kingdom of God to a kernel of wheat.

As I talked to Kelly's mom, I remembered that Kelly was one of the girls I not only drove places but also listened to, prayed for, and loved. God used me to share Christ with her, and she died loving Jesus. I realized that for all those years behind the wheel of my car I had no greater purpose.

I had asked God to give me a grand purpose, and he did.

While driving girls all over central Florida wasn't lofty, it *was* heavenly. And although it wasn't what I would have chosen, it turned out to be what I will always cherish.

NANCY KENNEDY

The 12 Days of Healing

A mystery giver brought balm for my grief.

We needed a miracle; that much was obvious. The summer of 1995 had been glorious…warm and full of picnics, evening walks with my husband, and family: my three girls, the grandkids, and my son. But in September, there was a knock on the door in the early morning hours.

"Mr. and Mrs. Harvey?" the young deputy sheriff had said. "There's no easy way to say this. There's been a shooting. It's Chad. He's dead."

Our 20-year-old son was dead—murdered just three blocks from our home. A crazed acquaintance, possibly in a jealous rage over his wife's attention to Chad, had shot him after a party. We stumbled through the funeral and the court appearances. We leafed through the sympathy cards and folded Chad's clothes to store them away. The nights grew colder, and the wind and snow came. Suddenly it was Christmas.

I was miserable. All around me there were carols being sung. Nativity scenes sprang up on lawns in our neighborhood, and the television schedule was punctuated with Christmas specials. I didn't even notice the TV though. I spent my evenings sitting on the couch crying and brooding. God had failed me. I had trusted him, and he hadn't come through.

Oh, I didn't think he did it on purpose. He just wasn't able to keep that man from killing my son. But I wished that he had been more honest about it to begin with and that he hadn't promised to answer my prayers if he couldn't do it. I stopped eating and lost 30 pounds. I began to be disappointed when I awoke in the mornings…still alive and doomed to live through another day. I wanted nothing so much as I wanted to die.

And it was Christmas. Feeling the way I did about God, clutching such anger to me and hunkering down against the world, I don't know why I prayed the prayer I did. But one night I lifted my tear-fogged eyes to heaven and said, "God, if you care about me, I need a miracle. Otherwise, I think I'll probably die."

"What kind of a miracle did you ask God for?" my husband, Charlie, asked.

"I don't know, but I'll know it when it comes."

I had given up trying to sing, although I'd always loved it. Singing was Chad's thing. Music was Chad's thing. When he died, all the music seemed to evaporate from my dry soul. I went out to the cemetery to try to sing a lullaby to my boy, but only a small, sad squeak came out of my throat.

It all seemed so futile. I had faith that Chad was in God's hands. I knew Chad hadn't ceased to exist, but I also knew I couldn't get to him, and I wanted to…desperately. People would tell me that someday I would see Chad again. I knew that; someday wasn't soon enough. Charlie reminded me that I still had him and the girls to live for. I knew what I had left, but what I had lost seemed to swallow everything.

One evening before Christmas, I was sitting huddled on the living room couch when there was a knock on the door. My 13-year-old daughter, Sarah, went to answer it.

"There's no one there," Sarah said. "But look what I found."

She held up a silly-looking centerpiece of evergreen branches and green apples with a plastic bluebird perched on top. Attached was a note: "'On the first day of Christmas, my true love gave to me a partridge in a pear tree.' We couldn't find a partridge, and our pear tree died, so you'll have to settle for a bluebird in an apple tree."

On another piece of paper was a segment of Scripture about the announcement of John the Baptist's birth. Nothing else. No name or address or clue of where the package came from. We sat dumbfounded.

"Could someone be doing 'The Twelve Days of Christmas' for us?" I wondered aloud.

"I always hated that song," Sarah said.

I had too. But this was different. We brainstormed, trying to guess who might be responsible for our surprise. We eliminated almost everyone. Finally we gave up and went to bed. Sleep didn't come easily. There were too many questions.

The next night we sat in the living room waiting. The television was on, and every time we thought we heard a sound, Charlie hit the mute button and we listened.

"This is really odd. I feel funny," I told Charlie. "I don't know what it is."

"I think it's anticipation," Charlie answered.

Yes, that's what it was. For so long we had been just surviving day to day, not looking forward to anything. Yet here we were, waiting for a knock on the door. It didn't come at eight p.m., at nine, or at ten. None of us wanted to admit how disappointed we were. We made excuses to stay up just a little longer. Suddenly there was a loud rap at the front door, and Sarah jumped up, nearly knocking over the coffee table.

She opened the door and pulled in another package. It was a box of Turtle candy with two Dove bars fastened to the top.

"On the second day of Christmas, my true love sent to me two turtledoves…"

This time the Scripture told of the angel Gabriel's appearance to the virgin Mary. Something began to stir inside me. I began to suspect that this was God's answer to my prayer. This was my miracle. Somehow he had laid it on someone's heart to do this thing that was so incredibly…*right*.

The third day of Christmas brought three French hens in the form of three Cornish hens (their French cousins had lost their passports, the note explained).

The fourth day was the date for our support group meeting. We sat in a circle at Parents of Murdered Children and told them our story; someone was going to such trouble to remind us of something I had forgotten. God still loved me. The group caught the excitement. Some of them were laughing, and some cried. I think maybe they had forgotten too.

We could barely wait to get home to see what the fourth day had brought us. When we drove up to our house though, we saw only our dog, Happy, lying on the porch, her eyes glinting in the light of the corner streetlight.

As Charlie reached the step, he kicked a small package. It was a cassette tape. Sarah raced to get her boom box, and we slipped the tape in to play it. It had three songs: "Surfin' Bird" by the Trashmen, "Tennessee Bird Walk" by Blanchard and Morgan, and "Turn, Turn, Turn" by the Byrds. On top of the package was taped a telephone calling card. The fourth day of Christmas—four calling birds. We sang along as the songs blasted from the tape player at two a.m. Who needed sleep?

The surprises continued over the next eight nights. Five golden rings were freshly fried doughnuts. Six geese a-laying were wonderful pastel chalk eggs. Seven swans swam across the top of a blue-frosted cake. Eight maids a-milking became a Holstein cow candle.

Eighteen ginger-people decorated as dancers peeked from the package on the ninth day. It seems the Equal Opportunity Employment Act wouldn't allow them to send just nine ladies dancing. The tenth day of Christmas we found ten wooden leaping puppets. On the eleventh, instead of eleven pipers piping, we found a James Galway tape, and on the twelfth day of Christmas there were twelve drums made out of cleverly frosted Oreos. Always, there was a portion of Scripture preparing us for the holiday to come.

Suddenly it occurred to me that I was looking forward to the next day and to life itself.

My miracle. When I couldn't talk to God, when I didn't even want to talk to him, he sent my miracle through someone else. Anonymously. We finally found out who our secret benefactors had been. We were grateful that they had been willing to let God use them.

My miracle. God used earthly hands to send it to me, but his fingerprints were all over it.

CARYL A. HARVEY

An Undeliverable Mother's Day Card

Sometimes life sends us a reminder that each day is a gift.

A few years ago, I somehow ended up buying two Mother's Day cards. I sent one to my mother, and because I keep a three-year calendar, I filed the other one away in the May section of the next year. Sadly, my mother died shortly after I sent that first card. Now I have a greeting card that can never be delivered—unless the US postal service can find a way to get it to eternity!

The more I've reflected on this undeliverable card, the more I've realized how it mirrors so much of life. Some situations prevent us from ever again doing what we originally intended. We can't hold on to the past regardless of how much we may want to. A loved one dies, and we grieve that we will never again hear her comforting, loving voice. Disease creeps in and robs us of the ability to do what we once enjoyed. An accident occurs, and in the blink of an eye, we lose abilities that we took for granted. These situations have an almost unbearable sense of finality.

Finality is a hard word to say. In fact, we spend a great deal of energy trying to find ways around it. We play the "if only" game: If only I try harder, it might get better. If only I act better, maybe there's still a chance. If only I pray harder, he might make it. But even prayer won't change some situations. My mother is gone, and the most fervent prayer won't bring her back. But prayer *will* help me to remember that life is short and that I need to live a life of love while I can. I'm reminded that I should be grateful for what I have now because it could be gone before I open next year's calendar.

So love now. Enjoy today. Be grateful this instant. Squeeze every drop of joy from each day. Pray hard and love deeply. And if you can, send your mom a Mother's Day card.

DON AYCOCK

God Speaks Through Unlikely People

*What could a severely challenged person possibly
have to say to an elite group of doctors?*

Henri Nouwen was a priest and a brilliant teacher at places like Harvard and Yale. Feeling led by God, he spent the last decade of his life serving a community of people with severe emotional, mental, and physical disabilities. It was an enormously healing time for him. In one of his many books, Henri tells a story about Trevor, a man with serious mental and emotional challenges who was sent by Henri's community to a psychiatric facility for evaluation. Henri wanted to see him, so he called the hospital to arrange a visit. When the hospital officials found out that Henri Nouwen was coming, they asked if they could have a lunch with him in the Golden Room—a special meeting room at the facility. They would also invite doctors and clergy people to the special luncheon. Henri agreed.

When Henri arrived, they took him to the Golden Room, but Trevor was nowhere to be seen. Troubled, Henri asked about Trevor's whereabouts. "Trevor cannot come to lunch," he was told. "Patients and staff are not allowed to have lunch together. Besides, no patient has ever had lunch in the Golden Room."

By nature, Henri was not a confrontational person. He was a meek man. But being guided by the Spirit, he sensed a directive: *Include Trevor.* Knowing that community is about inclusion, Henri thought, *Trevor ought to be here.* So Henri turned to the person in authority and said, "But the whole purpose of my coming was to have lunch with Trevor. If Trevor is not allowed to attend the lunch, I cannot attend either."

The thought of missing an opportunity for lunch with Henri Nouwen was too much. They soon found a way for Trevor to attend. When they all gathered together, something interesting happened. At one point during the lunch, Henri was talking to the person on his right and didn't notice that Trevor had stood up and lifted his glass of Coca-Cola.

"A toast. I will now offer a toast," Trevor said to the group.

Everybody in the room got nervous. What was he going to do?

Then Trevor, a deeply challenged man in a roomful of PhDs, started to sing, "If you're happy and you know it, raise your glass. If you're happy and you know it, raise your glass…"

Nobody was sure what to do. It was awkward. This man was challenged and broken beyond their understanding, yet he was beaming. He was thrilled to be there. So they started to sing, softly at first and then louder and louder until doctors and clergymen and Henri Nouwen were all practically shouting, "If you're happy and you know it, raise your glass."

Henri went on to give a talk at the luncheon, but everybody remembered the moment God spoke most clearly—through someone they all would have said was the least likely person.

JOHN ORTBERG

Learning to Apologize

Even our flawed attempts can lead to healing.

From babyhood, my daughter Lulu has steadfastly obeyed the apostle Paul's command, "Do not let the sun go down while you are still angry" (Ephesians 4:26). She must have learned the passage in one of her first Sunday school classes. Somehow, the command's urgency gripped her baby brain with the fear that whoever had angered her—usually me—might die in the night and she'd be left knowing that her last feelings had been angry and that the last words reverberating between us into eternity were hurtful or mean.

Consequently, to this day, whenever we have a conflict, Lulu shows up at my side shortly before bedtime with the demand that I apologize so she can sleep.

"You have to say you're sorry," she rages, her 14-year-old face stony and closed, her body as taut and resistant as an angry toddler's.

The conflict is rarely my fault. Lulu has a formidable temper and often seems to invent offenses. Sometimes I have no idea what's upset her. Other times, a minor misunderstanding becomes infected with adolescent crankiness and is swollen out of proportion into yet another felony on my bad parenting record.

Over the years, though, I've come to understand that Lulu's demand for me to say I'm sorry is her particular brand of apology. A mediocre one, admittedly—although better than some, and certainly better than none at all. She does yield enough to come find me. Or, if not—if she's so mad she stews in her room until my tentative knock on her door—I still know she values my love enough to desire reconciliation. She awaits it and can't sleep without it. *This desire amounts to a kind of repentance,* I remind myself, and everything in me longs to forgive.

Nevertheless, sometimes I struggle to eke out the demanded apology. To own fault for something I'm certain I didn't do. To claim responsibility for a slight I never intended. To get inside Lulu's hurt or impatience or expectations deeply enough to glimpse myself from her perspective and see my error. To recognize my own impatience or self-centeredness or stress usually lurking beneath the perceived offense. To confess it.

I always manage, though. I search my soul and offer her the best apology I can muster. "I should have known..." I tell her. "I didn't mean to...I'm sorry. I'll never do it again." Bad parenting, I know. Insufficiently authoritative and just. Certainly far too accommodating to a fuming, wrongheaded teenager hungry for power. But I, too, want to sleep.

So in the interest of sleep or love—or perhaps even in pursuit of the One who promises both—I forgive Lulu's absurd demand and offer the words she wants. "I shouldn't have. I failed you. I'm sorry." I consider these words, wrung from my righteous heart, a small contribution to our relationship. And invariably, in the moment of giving them voice, I find myself genuinely, miraculously repentant—and better equipped to love and understand her. Our mutual apologies heal more than just the conflict in question.

Since becoming a Christian a dozen years ago, I've heard many sermons promoting forgiveness but none promoting apology. I've always wondered why not. The two topics are certainly related. A good apology—one involving the offender's deep introspection and admission of guilt—frequently has the amazing power to *activate* forgiveness. And true forgiveness, not merely the forgiver's relinquishment of resentment but the genuine reconciliation of both parties, usually hinges upon an apology. Without it, reconciliation often isn't an option.

Unlike forgiving—especially the extreme mandate that believers follow God's example and forgive even in the absence of repentance—apologizing is necessarily a two-way enterprise. An apology can't occur without both offender and forgiver present. Even the worst apologies—such as disguised counteraccusations or veiled rationalizations—bring the conflicting parties together with the shared goal of reconciliation. If I refuse to apologize when Lulu comes to me, she and I are nevertheless in one place, facing each other, openly acknowledging our conflict and our shared desire for release from it. Before words emerge from our mouths, we've both already invested something in reconciliation: Lulu, the coming, and I, the acknowledging. And we both stand to win if the apology succeeds.

Bad apologies, however, come much more readily than good ones. It's easy to say I didn't mean it or that Lulu misunderstood me. Or to simply claim it didn't happen the way she says it did. Such conditional apologies merely slow the forgiving and delay the potential reconciliation. And they delay sleep.

Unless I consciously set out to do so—as I've learned to do in my conflicts with Lulu—I almost never manage a guilt admission unsullied by accusations or rationalizations. If I'm at odds with my husband or a coworker or a friend, I struggle to look past my own understanding of the conflict and see myself from the other's side. And even when I scrutinize my actions, I often overlook the most obvious evidence of my amazing power to hurt and upset others. The acidic tone half-buried in pretended humor. The subliminal meanness. The myriad species of hate generated by my arrogance.

Lulu must also learn how to apologize—to substitute *I* statements for the easier *you* statements—and to consider my perspective as well as her own. And someday I'll teach her. For now, though, I simply model my best apology, which occasionally elicits a tiny apology in return, along with the soothing balm of mutual forgiveness.

And for all Lulu's faults—for all mine—I take comfort that Lulu still hugs me goodnight at bedtime and that her last words to me, should I have the good fortune to die in my sleep, will have been "I love you."

Patty Kirk

Memories of Mom

*How one woman found love in the present, joy
in the past, and hope in the future.*

Mom grew up around the coal mines where her daddy worked, deep in the mountains of Virginia. She came from a large, poverty-stricken family, so she learned how to be content with little.

Dad and Mom were also poor by the world's standards, but as a kid growing up, I didn't know it. We were rich in so many other ways. Dad worked two or three jobs at a time so Mom could stay home with her five children. She hummed softly as she went about her work. It was as if she had blocked out all the bad news and was contemplating what was good and right and lovely. She always lived in the present, fondly reflecting on the past and looking forward to the future. She found love in the present, joy in the past, and hope in the future.

I will never forget the day doctors told us that Mom had terminal cancer. I was devastated by the news. Things did not seem to change for Mom, though. Whenever I visited her, she was busy cooking or baking, doing a load of clothes, sewing, or working on something else. As she worked, she hummed a beautiful tune.

When I spoke with her about the cancer, she was calm. She told me that this was not really her home. She said that she had a home in heaven and that she would be going there soon. She told me not to worry because she would be all right. Although that brought tears to my eyes, she continued to hum. I saw a beauty in my mother that I had never seen before. In her affliction she had become radiant.

When my mother died, she was 59 years old. I have replayed her words many times: "This is not my home. I have a home in heaven. I'll be all right."

Now I'm a pastor, and I've seen many people, like Mom, go to another home. As I minister to them, I am reminded of her—afflicted and yet radiant.

BILL FIX

Our Divine Distortion

We can't see God clearly without Jesus. O come, Emmanuel.

When I found a brand-new laptop for half price on eBay, I told my friend and musical colleague Spencer about my bargain of a find. He was worried: "Usually when something's too good to be true…"

"I know," I replied impatiently, "but the seller has a 100 percent approval rating."

"Be careful," warned Spencer.

"Of course," I assured him, annoyed. I wasn't born yesterday.

I sent the seller $1300 and discovered in very short, sickening order that I had fallen prey to a classic scam. A fraudster had hacked someone's eBay identity in order to relieve easy marks like me of our money.

I felt an absolute fool—and didn't want to tell Spencer. The next time I saw his number on my caller ID, I didn't answer. I could just imagine his "I told you so."

Soon, I was avoiding Spencer completely. And I started to resent him. Why did he have to be so judgmental? Why couldn't he be on my side? Why was I ever friends with that jerk?

Eventually, we had to fly together to perform at a concert. "Whatever happened with that computer thing?" he asked an hour into the flight. Cornered, I finally confessed my foolishness, dreading the inevitable response. But as soon as I told Spencer about my mistake, a strange thing happened. The enemy I had turned him into evaporated. Spencer turned into Spencer again, my teasing but deeply empathetic buddy.

As embarrassed as I was by my eBay error, I felt even dumber about the way I had allowed my shame to distort my perception of a best friend. If my hand had not been forced, I would have remained estranged from him indefinitely.

I've always considered myself perceptive, but the longer I live, the more I discover my susceptibility to misinterpretation. This is true of the way I view my friends, truer of the way I see my enemies, and perhaps truest of the way I perceive God.

I was raised to understand that sin's gravest consequence is the way it forces God to perceive me: *God is holy, I'm not, and there's no way he can even look at me until I have the covering of Christ's blood.* In my teens, I clipped a poem out of a youth magazine in which the poet asks—and answers—a pressing question: "How can a righteous God look at me, a sinner, and see a precious child? Simple: The Son gets in his eyes."

But what about how I look at God? I've often been oblivious to one of the most insidious by-products of the fall: Sin affects my perception of God. Or, to turn a phrase from that poem, *the sin gets in my eyes*.

Before Adam and Eve had fallen for the first lie, they basked in God's company. But after a few bites of forbidden fruit, they no longer looked forward to seeing their Maker. When he came calling, they hid.

Had God changed? No. Adam and Eve's brokenness altered their perception of God, not his character. Ever since, we humans have been letting our shame poison our understanding of God. He becomes an ogre, or a bookkeeper, or maybe just a disinterested, detached monarch.

Many of us unconsciously relate to God our Father as a Godfather—there's a lot he can do for us when he likes us, but don't get on his bad side. So we avoid him. And the longer we refuse to take his calls, the worse the distortion becomes.

But here is some good news: Jesus is the antidote to our misperceptions. When we speak of the Incarnation, we acknowledge that Jesus is "God con carne"—God with meat on. Our questions about God's character—*Is he really about mercy, justice, and a love that just won't quit?*—are answered in the person of Jesus.

In one sense, Adam and Eve were right to fear facing God. The consequences of their choices were painful. But even God's seemingly harshest judgment—banishment from the garden and the tree of life—was rooted in love. If the first humans had accessed eternal life in Eden, they would have remained in their brokenness forever. God chose another way—a death and resurrection way that would cost him much—because he was and is and always will be with us and for us. Yes, we should fear sin's consequences. But we need not fear the perfect love of a God willing to come and shiver in our skin to save us.

We do not have the power to change God's character. Our Father is our Father. Always has been, always will be. But we will never see him for who he really is until the Son gets in our eyes.

CAROLYN ARENDS

Potty Break

What I really want for my fortieth birthday.

I turn 40 this year, and I'm just waiting for my husband to ask me what I want for my birthday. I've got my answer all prepared. It's probably not what he expects though. In the years before kids, he'd have gotten off easy with jewelry or clothes, dinner out, and a gift certificate to a day spa.

But after ten years and four kids, my idea of the perfect birthday gift has evolved. What I really want this year is four hours in my own bathroom alone and uninterrupted. Just peace and quiet and porcelain.

I suppose this makes me a cheap date, but after ten years of doing whatever I've got to do in the bathroom in front of an audience, four hours of bathroom solitude sounds better than anything he can charge on his MasterCard or wrap in black "Over the Hill" gift wrap.

My birthday fantasy looks like this—me loitering in the tub with my eyes closed. Around me there are no action figures, no stick-on alphabet letters, no naked Barbies. (Talk about depressing. The *last* thing I need when I'm bent over shaving my legs is a naked Barbie smirking at me.)

I want no little urchins there to offer commentary on my breasts or belly or buttocks. I don't want to hear that I'm getting fat but "Don't worry, Mommy, you look good that way," or "Hey, the water goes *way* down when you get out."

I want to shave my legs without delivering a safety lecture about my razor. I don't want to share my shaving cream with anyone, no matter how much fun the stuff is. I want to fog up the mirror without having to peek around the shower curtain when somebody asks, "What letter is this, Mommy?" I want the curtain to stay shut and not be fanned open every few seconds, inspiring me to once again explain that shower curtains are for keeping water *off* the floor.

I want to let the water get as hot as I can stand it. I don't want to hear that anyone is taking up all the room; *I* want all the room. I especially don't want to hear, "Oops! Guess I forgot to tinkle before I got in the tub." I want to stretch my legs without it being seen as an invitation for a pony ride. I want to towel off without having to teach an anatomy lesson titled "Why Mommy Looks Different than Daddy."

And while I'm at it, I want to do what I need to on the toilet without spectators. I don't want to have to remember who tore off the toilet paper for me the last time so I'm sure everyone gets their turn. I want to pick up a magazine, read an article from start to finish, and actually comprehend what I'm reading. I want to close the door and not have little notes slid underneath with my name on them or see tiny fingers wiggling up at me.

Then I want to paint my nails—only mine, no one else's. I don't want to have the "But, sweetie, nail polish is only for girls and mommies, not boys" talk, which is usually followed that evening by the "Oh, honey, I only did his toenails" talk. I want to give myself a pedicure and facial and touch up my roots without once stopping to yell, "I'm in the bathroom. No, I can't come to you; you come to me!"

I don't care where my husband takes the kids. He'll think of something. I just want four hours to luxuriate in my own bathroom alone! I hope that while my husband is sitting in the McDonald's play yard staring at his watch, he'll remember he's turning 50 this year. Perhaps I'll tell him I'm toying with the idea of declaring the remote control off-limits to anyone but Dad for that long, glorious afternoon. Consider the possibilities!

MIMI GREENWOOD KNIGHT

Priceless Trust

What could be more valuable than knowing
that God watches over our loved ones?

Only my daughter Laura has the power to get me to eat a raw quail egg.

We did so at our favorite sushi restaurant in Charlotte, North Carolina, where she lives. I'd come from my home in Florida to speak at a conference and had only a few short hours to spend with her.

It's been five years since she moved away from home, and I think I've finally, finally, finally (maybe) stopped thinking of her as a feral child who needs me to hover over her and guide her every move, breath, decision, and thought.

She's 25 now, capable, making more money than I am, going to school, and dating a guy who treats her well.

One thing I noticed on this trip: The older she gets, the better we seem to get along. Maybe it's because I no longer fret over whether or not she's paid her bills or cleaned her bathroom. Maybe it's because she sees my wrinkles and graying hair and takes pity on her dear old mom.

Maybe it's a little of both, or maybe it's something altogether different. I don't want to analyze it to death—I'd rather enjoy the too few times we're together.

Laura is my prodigal. Of my two daughters, she caused me to shed the most tears. Although I love them both and couldn't choose one child over the other, my heart has always been most tender toward Laura.

I think crying and pleading with God over a wayward child either makes your heart hardened from self-protection or tenderized, like a piece of steak that's been whacked repeatedly with a mallet.

The hardest thing my husband and I ever had to do was tell Laura she had to leave our home. She was about 18 and out of control, and she moved in with people who turned out to be drug addicts and thieves. They stole her clothes, her camera, and her money. She slept in fear in a strange bed as I slept at home in grief and worry, missing my child, afraid to let God do the work he had to do in both of our lives.

But God was faithful.

Near the entrance to the apartment complex where she lived, a giant billboard shouted, Jesus Is Real. Months later, Laura told me that every day when she saw that sign she'd think, *I don't know how, but I bet my mom is behind that.* I wasn't, but God was.

Another time, while visiting a friend out of state, she went to a rock concert to hear a group whose song lyrics she knew were beyond blasphemous.

When I picked her up from the airport, she told me about the concert and that her eyes were opened to evil, that it's both compelling and repulsive. She felt pulled, she said.

Then she told me about a guy who stood near her the whole time, not saying anything, wearing a bright yellow T-shirt with *Jesus* written across the front.

"Who goes to a concert wearing a bright yellow Jesus shirt?" she asked.

I didn't tell her what I knew to be true—that God had sent someone to remind my daughter that Jesus is real, that she's his and he won't let her go.

He's done that over and over and over.

Sometimes she tells me of these "God things," and sometimes I find out other ways. Mostly, I imagine, I don't know half of it. But I know enough to know that I truly can trust him with her, which sounds simple but is not easy.

That night as Laura and I ate sushi, we chitchatted about nothing special. I might have liked to dispense my mom-nags (as my unsolicited advice is called) between bites, but it wasn't the time or place.

Besides, for the first time since she's been gone, I realized I didn't have to. She's not the kid who left home five years ago, and even if she doesn't recognize or welcome it at this point, Jesus is real in her life, and he's way more capable than I am to take care of her—and I *can* trust him.

Plane ticket to Charlotte: $398. Sushi with Laura: $47. Being reminded of God's faithfulness and eating a raw quail egg: priceless.

NANCY KENNEDY

Tattle Tales

My husband ate my lunch!

One Sunday afternoon I sautéed some matchstick carrots, sliced sweet onion and mushrooms, seasoned it with garlic, red pepper flakes, and Parmesan cheese, put it all in a plastic container, and put it in the fridge for my lunch on Monday.

Sometime between putting it in the fridge Sunday and seeing the empty container in the sink Monday morning, I realized my husband ate it.

He ate it *all*. My lunch. *My* lunch.

He ate my lunch!

In his defense, I didn't tell him it was my lunch; I didn't put a sticky note on it saying, "Don't eat this."

On Saturday I'd made some macaroni salad and put it in an identical plastic container. He ate from that and I didn't say anything, so I'm sure Barry thought everything in a plastic container was fair game.

But it wasn't. That was my lunch—and he ate it!

I wasn't so much angry as I was amused, in a ticked-off way, if you can imagine that. However, I acted as if I'd been Wronged. Violated. Put Out and Put Upon. I wanted vengeance and justice! So I posted my grievance on my Facebook page: My husband ate my lunch!

Next, I text messaged my daughters: *Your* dad ate my lunch!

Then I went to work and, hanging my head, bemoaned to my friends, "Sorry, I can't eat lunch with you today. My husband ate mine."

Everyone I told commiserated with me. *Oh, you poor thing. How tragic. What a terrible, terrible husband. You, among all women, have suffered greatly.*

I felt like a victim all day and enjoyed the sympathetic pity immensely.

Of course, I'm being facetious, although I truly did make a big show out of tattling on my husband. But mostly I was goofing around—that time.

I'm ashamed to say there have been other times when I've tattled on my husband out of anger, spitefully wanting to be seen as more right or righteous than he is.

At one time I freely aired my husband's dirty laundry to anyone who would listen. If he had hurt me in any way, if he had failed to live up to my expectations, if he did or said something I thought he shouldn't, it was nothing for me to pick up the phone and call a friend.

Oh, I'd preface it by saying, "We need to pray," but my true motivation was always to tattle on my husband.

My wake-up call came the day I overheard a former pastor's wife telling someone how tired she gets of hearing women talk negatively about their husbands. "By the time I meet these guys, I already hate them," she said.

I felt my face flush with shame. She could have been thinking of me when she said that. I'd cornered her many times with stories of my husband's so-called atrocities.

Hearing her words was like God whacking me with a tire iron. I was instantly ashamed at how often I had disrespected my husband and maligned his character by my careless words. I begged God to change me, to give me a chance to do it right.

James says, "It only takes a spark, remember, to set off a forest fire. A careless or wrongly placed word out of your mouth can do that. By our speech we can ruin the world, turn harmony to chaos, throw mud on a reputation, send the whole world up in smoke and go up in smoke with it, smoke right from the pit of hell" (James 3:5-6 MSG).

I've never forgotten my pastor's wife's words, nor have I forgotten the biblical warnings of James, and in the past 20 or so years I've tried my best not to bad-mouth my husband. I think I do okay.

I know one thing for certain: My husband never talks badly about me. People tell me that all the time. My goal and desire is to have people tell him that about me.

By the way, my husband and I celebrated our thirty-fourth anniversary this past Sunday. He bought me lunch.

NANCY KENNEDY

Good News in the Bad News

A reminder of the power of adversity to change our lives.

Psychologist Jonathon Haidt suggested a hypothetical exercise: Imagine that you have a child, and for five minutes you're given a script of what will be that child's life. You get an eraser. You can edit it. You can take out whatever you want.

You read that your child will have a learning disability in grade school. Reading, which comes easily for some kids, will be laborious for yours. In high school, your kid will make a great circle of friends; then one of them will die of cancer. After high school this child will actually get into the college he wanted to attend. While there, your child will be in a car crash, lose a leg, and go through a difficult depression. A few years later, your child will get a great job but then lose that job in an economic downturn. Your child will get married but later go through the grief of separation.

You get this script for your child's life and have five minutes to edit it. What would you erase? Wouldn't you want to take out all the stuff that would cause him pain?

I am part of a generation of "helicopter parents." We're constantly trying to swoop into our kids' lives and make sure no one is mistreating them, no one is disappointing them. We want them to experience one unobstructed success after another.

One Halloween a mom came to our door to trick or treat. Why didn't she send her kid? Well, the weather's a little bad, she said; she was driving so he didn't have to walk in the mist. But why not send him to the door? Well, he had fallen asleep in the car, she said, so she didn't want him to have to wake up. I felt like saying, "Why don't you eat all his candy and get his stomachache for him too—then he can be completely protected!"

If you could wave a wand, if you could erase every failure, setback, suffering, and pain, are you sure it would be a good idea? Would it cause your child to grow up to be a better, stronger, more generous person? Is it possible that in some way people actually need adversity, setbacks, and maybe even trauma to reach the fullest level of development and growth?

JOHN ORTBERG

There Goes the Neighborhood

Do I have to love my neighbor if he breaks the law?

We used to live on a street in Surrey, British Columbia, we called the Mother of All Cul-de-Sacs. The spaces between the houses were large enough to accommodate a dozen parked cars or a spirited soccer match. Our daughter learned to walk in that cul-de-sac, and our son shot his first basket into a full-sized hoop there. (Granted, he was on his father's shoulders at the time.) Every night, a dozen kids would spill onto the street with bikes or hockey sticks, and we would congratulate ourselves on having selected the perfect neighborhood.

A year after we moved in, the street's complexion changed. Several of the young families moved away, and we had a hard time getting to know our new neighbors.

We heard nasty rumors that certain residents were using their homes to grow marijuana. "Grow-ops" were a rampant problem in our area, but my husband and I doubted we were sharing fences with criminals. Our friendly neighbor to the right, "Van," had recently arrived in Canada but was working hard on his English. Our neighbors to the left, an older couple who gardened relentlessly, seemed reserved but agreeable.

One afternoon, my kids and I noticed a flurry of activity. We watched as our neighbors on both sides were chased and cuffed by police, and truckloads of plants and equipment were pulled out of each of their residences. A sign declaring the area to be the site of a successful drug bust was proudly displayed—in *our* driveway!

My husband arrived home and intercepted one of the officers walking across our lawn. Our four-year-old eavesdropped on their conversation and ran back to me. "Our neighbors were arrested for *throwing dough,*" he said, confused and troubled. "Why aren't you allowed to throw dough?" I wasn't sure whether to clarify that the officer had actually said "growing dope."

That night, the more I wrestled with how to explain the day's events to our kids, the angrier I got. How *dare* those people invade our neighborhood and expose our children to dangerous criminal elements?

I was still fuming the next day when I left to perform at an event called "Love Surrey." Area pastors had organized a multidenominational outdoor service in an effort to reach out to the community—just the sort of thing I love to support. But my anger boiled backstage as some friends warned me that grow-op owners are often quickly released and face minimal repercussions.

I returned home to see Van standing in the middle of our formerly kid-friendly cul-de-sac, holding a Coke can and chatting with my husband. I was seething when Mark walked into the house 30 minutes later.

"I can't *believe* he's a free man," I hissed.

"Yeah," Mark shrugged. "The laws are pretty weak. But…"

"But what?" I asked, incredulous.

"Van feels terrible." Mark sighed. "He's been out there pulling tiny weeds from the cul-de-sac garden, stuffing them into that Coke can. He's trying to show everyone how sorry he is. He keeps promising it will never happen again."

As Mark told me some of Van's story of personal tragedy, poor choices, and exploitation by people higher up the criminal food chain, I had a sudden epiphany.

Van was my *neighbor*.

Of course I knew he lived next door, but I realized with a start that Van was my neighbor in the "love your neighbor as yourself" sense. It dawned on me that if I had been the lawyer trying to define the law in Luke's Gospel, Jesus could have told me a story about a pot grower in Surrey.

I looked down at the new "Love Surrey" T-shirt I was wearing and winced, remembering Charles Schultz's ironic words: "I love mankind; it's just people I can't stand." I had known—preached, even—love of neighbor in the abstract. I had believed that the point of the Good Samaritan parable was that my neighbor is anyone who needs my help. But I had been thinking more of innocent victims in Africa than of drug-producing villains on my street.

I hope the kindness we eventually decided to show Van helped him change half as much as he changed the way we see the people around us. The driven professional with the BMW, the retiree with the yappy dog, the new immigrant too shy to make eye contact—these are our neighbors. And if we love the God who made them, we will love them as we love ourselves.

C.S. Lewis observed, "There are no ordinary people. You have never met a mere mortal." There are seven billion residents on this cul-de-sac we call home, each of them bearing the image of God, each of them a neighbor to be loved. We might as well start with the immortals next door.

CAROLYN ARENDS

There's a Party Going On!

And those who are inside can't wait for you to join them.

Why do Jesus and his angels rejoice over one repenting sinner? Can they see something we can't? Do they know something we don't? Absolutely. They know what heaven holds. They've seen the table, they've heard the music, and they can't wait to see your face when you arrive. Better still, they can't wait to see *you*.

When you arrive and enter the party, something wonderful will happen. A final transformation will occur. You will be just like Jesus.

Of all the blessings of heaven, one of the greatest will be you! You will be God's magnum opus, his work of art. The angels will gasp. God's work will be completed. At last, you will have a heart like his.

You will love with a perfect love.

You will worship with a radiant face.

You'll hear each word God speaks.

Your heart will be pure, your words will be like jewels, your thoughts will be like treasures.

You will be just like Jesus. You will, at long last, have a heart like his. Envision the heart of Jesus, and you'll be envisioning your own. Guiltless. Fearless. Thrilled and joyous. Tirelessly worshipping. Flawlessly discerning. As the mountain stream is pristine and endless, so will be your heart.

You will be like him.

And if that were not enough, everyone else will be like him as well. A famous preacher once said, "Heaven is the perfect place for people made perfect." Heaven is populated by those who let God change them. Arguments will cease, for jealousy won't exist. Suspicions won't surface,

for there will be no secrets. Every sin is gone. Every insecurity is forgotten. Every fear is past.

Pure wheat. No weeds.

Pure gold. No alloy.

Pure love. No lust.

Pure hope. No fear.

No wonder the angels rejoice when one sinner repents; they know
another work of art will soon grace the gallery of God. They know
what heaven holds.

MAX LUCADO

Truer Test of Love

Small decisions can make a big difference.

When it comes to decorating our house, my husband and I have a rule: The one who cares more about the decision gets to choose.

I made up that rule, and for more than 30 years it's worked for me—especially since my husband, Barry, never cared one way or another. However, now that Barry's retired and at home more, he suddenly cares deeply and passionately about things that never interested him before.

I'm not sure I like this new side of Barry!

I started noticing it after our youngest daughter had moved out and we turned her room into an office. I replaced the single bed with a daybed, found a drop-leaf table and painted it shiny black, bought a rustic desk with a hutch top, and hung a Lowell Herrero print on the wall. To my mind, this spare room is to be a showcase for my decorating taste—and oh, by the way, also an office.

Barry has completely different ideas about the spare room. To him, it's an office first. Therefore the paper shredder, just because it's an eyesore, shouldn't be relegated to the closet or garage. And the drop-leaf table is the perfect place for his monstrous calendar, piles of receipts, and boxes of paperclips and rubber bands. After all, he says, it's an office.

He also can't understand my choice of warm colors and lots of black. Barry prefers gray everything. Period. (I tell him gray is fine if you're a sweatshirt.) So he growls at my carefully arranged vignettes of black-and-white photos and etched glass vases and vintage books—all a mixture of texture and color on top of the desk hutch. To him, it's unnecessary clutter.

He doesn't think the daybed needs a dozen throw pillows. And although he does like the Lowell Herrero print, he'd like to hang the photo of his old softball team next to it, an idea that makes me shudder.

Then, the other day, Barry asked me to move a metal sculpture of a tree off the table in the entryway. That tree is one of my favorite things in the house—and one of Barry's least favorites. He'd kept catching his T-shirt sleeves on its branches, and he was afraid if he knocked it over, I'd blame him for breaking it on purpose.

But I decided to stand my ground. After all, the tree was a gift from a friend, and everyone (except Barry) loved it exactly where I'd put it. I tried moving it to the top of the bookcase in the living room and then to another table, but the tree looked good only on that half-circle table in the entryway—so I put the sculpture back.

I felt convicted, however, when we looked at paint for the bathroom earlier today. As I gathered samples of willow herb green and chickadee yellow, Barry went for the antique- and off-whites. He believes that if God had intended walls to be willow herb or chickadee, he wouldn't have created antique-white paint. Barry's adamancy about that, too, makes me crazy.

But according to my rule, the one for whom the decision means the most gets to choose. So far it's always been me, but apparently things are changing. Lately that person's been Barry, and in the grand scheme, what does it matter?

Besides, love is not self-seeking, as the apostle Paul says in 1 Corinthians 13:5. Love doesn't demand or whine or make life generally unpleasant. Love doesn't belittle or make fun of another person's tastes, even if they're different. Yet I'm ashamed to admit I've been guilty of all those unlovely characteristics more times than I can count.

It's easy to show grand gestures of love. To say the words, write the poems, stand with another in the storm. But the little things—the petty irritants and odd quirks that get under the skin and fester—are often a truer test of love.

So this afternoon, I put my tree sculpture on the bookcase and took down some of the stuff collecting dust on the desk hutch.

And it felt good—surprisingly, even better than getting my own way.

NANCY KENNEDY

Worried About Worrying

Perhaps a little anxiety can be a good thing.

My daughter Charlotte just got her driver's license and first car. It's been a rocky time for me. Keeping track of where she is. Making sure she doesn't use her phone while she's driving. Struggling not only to accept but also to embrace her acceleration toward independence. Worrying.

Yesterday she drove 40 miles to Barnes & Noble. Her goal was to go that far alone, to cross "the big road" into their parking lot (highways terrify her), to order a grande Earl Grey tea, to read in one of their dingy armchairs, and then to come home. All innocent desires. And at least midway through her adventure, I knew she was fine, because my husband, Kris, and I met up with her briefly at the bookstore, where we always go at the end of our weekly date. Still, I worried the whole way home. When police sent us around an accident, I was sure it was Charlotte and made Kris defy the law and bypass the detour to see.

Meanwhile, our younger daughter, Lulu, is a thousand miles away attending what she calls "nerd camp": a college course for high schoolers on politics and literature. So far, it's been mostly about existentialism. They're reading bleak novels arguing that God doesn't exist and only personal choice matters.

"They're so depressing," Lulu told me, "they make me want to go to church."

That statement was startling from a kid who's been unenthusiastic about church of late, maybe because she's 14, or maybe because our family's been visiting different churches for a while looking for one that pleases us all equally—for a church, in other words, that doesn't exist. Wherever we go, both girls act bored during the service and criticize everything afterward. Soon, they'll be on their own and may not attend church at all, and I wrestle with the worries I share with all parents of children who are apathetic about church: *Does God matter to them? Do they sense his presence in their lives? Will they abandon not just church but God himself as they escape further and further into a world beyond my influence or control?*

Worrying is a sin, my Christian friends always tell me. They point to angels who always seem to be saying, "Fear not!" and they quote Paul's famous advice from his prison cell: "Do not be anxious about anything, but in every situation, by prayer and petition, with thanksgiving, present your requests to God. And the peace of God, which transcends all understanding, will guard your hearts and your minds in Christ Jesus" (Philippians 4:6-7). My friends think we should be like Paul: "content in any and every situation" (Philippians 4:12).

I tell my friends that worrying is a way of praying. I even have a name for it: pray-worrying. Indeed, what is praying but giving voice to worries as a means of seeking that elusive peace Paul promises God will send?

Nevertheless, I've secretly added worrying itself to my list of worries. I know I worry too much. Not only about dramatic disasters, like Charlotte being in a terrible car accident, but also about my daughters coming under the tutelage of ardent atheists or questioning matters of faith or making bad choices in life.

I worry, in short, about my daughters growing up—when growing up is exactly what teenagers should be doing. *How awful it would be if they* weren't *growing up,* I remind myself, suddenly thankful. *What if they* weren't *making choices, good or bad, but were just waiting—like newborns, like our dogs—for me to decide everything for them? What if they* weren't *asking questions about faith? What if they didn't care about faith at all?*

God's plan is for us to grow up. To step out from where we start, even though doing so inevitably means making mistakes. To grow up is to question everything and pursue faith, not from habit or compulsion but from free will.

Allowing one's children to grow up and find faith on their own is, I'm thinking, the crux of Jesus's parable of the prodigal son. It's always perplexed me that the father—who represents God in the story—gives his son the inheritance in the first place. Any parenting book would say that indulging such greedy desires is a mistake—just as my sister told me that buying my daughter a car was a mistake, although a car is a virtual necessity of growing up and working and being involved in activities in rural areas like ours.

"You're spoiling her!" my sister complained. And I worry she's right.

Either way, the father in Jesus's story sounds like the classic enabler, helping his son into a life of misery and sin. Various pastors have explained the story's purpose is not to model parenting but to illustrate salvation. I wonder, though.

Maybe God is showing me—through this story so real-sounding it could be from *my* life—that letting kids grow up means allowing them independence even though they will inevitably mess up. Perhaps it's okay to worry about them, just as that father in the parable surely does. When the prodigal son finally returns home, the father sees him while he's "still a long way off" (Luke 15:20). Clearly, the father has been searching the horizon, pray-worrying that his son will turn out all right. God himself worries about his children. Just before he destroyed most of earth's inhabitants in the flood, he looked down on them, and "his heart was deeply troubled" (Genesis 6:6).

I don't mean to defend worrying, but I do think it's unavoidable, in parenting at least. Perhaps worrying even plays a role in securing the contentment in all things Paul prescribes. His injunction against worrying is, after all, part of a larger message of thanks to the Philippians for *their* worries on his behalf: "I rejoiced greatly in the Lord that at last you renewed your concern for me" (Philippians 4:10).

Worrying can lead to action, as when the concerned Philippians sent Paul aid. Or worrying might lead to new insight, like my sudden thankfulness that my children *are* growing up. Certainly, as Paul suggests, we shouldn't wallow in anxiety, but rather step forth from our worries into faith. We should scan the horizon daily, hourly even, and know that God's will, his splendid purpose for each of us, will certainly come to pass.

PATTY KIRK

What the Chicken Told Me

God used an annoying rooster to shake me out of my foul mood.

It was my first day on the job as a financial specialist for a busy bank in Central Florida. I stood in my new office with the beautiful cherry furniture, a painting of the ocean, and a wall of windows looking out on green grass and trees. It was perfect.

Then I heard a rooster crow. Was I imagining it? There were no farms nearby. No, there it was again. It was definitely a rooster. And it was right outside my window. I had wanted to move out of the big city, but this was ridiculous. Had I moved to Green Acres? I looked outside on the grass, on the ground, in the trees...but no rooster was evident.

I told my coworker that I had a rooster crowing outside my window, and she just laughed. "Oh, that's the electric chicken at Barnhill's, the restaurant across the street," she said. We laughed and called it our pet chicken.

I laughed about it at first, but after hearing that chicken crow all day long, every day, it soon was not funny. I grew to hate that rooster. Every time it would crow, I'd say, "Darn that chicken!" And the more I hated it, the more it crowed. It seemed to crow relentlessly.

I wondered what caused him to crow. Was it the door opening? Did the staff hit a button every time they sold a chicken dinner? Did it crow every time they wrung a chicken's neck? Would they like me to wring a chicken's neck for them?

I was making myself crazy. It never occurred to me to go over and ask them why the rooster crowed, because when lunchtime came I wanted to get as far away from that bird as possible.

So I guess you could say this chicken was my thorn in the flesh. I would just have to bear it.

The job I had was difficult. I sold stocks, bonds, mutual funds, and annuities. I was a loan officer and a mortgage lender, and I had to open new accounts and do customer service. I dealt with difficult people and complex problems all day long. It stretched my mind and spirit to their limits. I had to call on God moment by moment just to stay in my seat and not run out the door. I learned a new level of patience and the meaning of longsuffering as I dealt with people who thought nothing of insulting me or cussing me out.

Until I went to work at that bank, I never realized how hard bank employees worked—and for so little pay. What's more, the threat of a robbery, though statistically remote, is always in the back of their minds.

It wasn't long before I knew this job was not for me. But I decided I would stick it out for a few more months until I paid off my bills. And so the problems remained of how to deal with the difficult people and the crowing chicken.

One day, it occurred to me that I could approach both of my problems in one of two ways. I didn't want to quit, so I could either grit my teeth and bear it or I could make the best of it somehow.

I asked God to show me how to handle my situation, and then I tried a new tactic. When the rooster crowed, I joked about it with my customers. When they would hear it for the first time, I'd tell them I'd pay for their dinner if they'd go over to Barnhill's and pluck that bird! I even had a contest to name him. The winner: Barnie, the Electric Chicken.

I had made my peace with Barnie at last. One day I heard him crow, and I swear he seemed to be saying, "I can do it for you." God was speaking to me through Barnie. After that, every time I heard Barnie crow I'd think, "God can help me get through this."

And he did. When Barnie crowed or the customers were mean, I'd hear that chicken speaking God's promise: "I can do it for you." And I'd instantly feel at ease. Time after time, God helped me be patient with unhappy customers or take the time to simply listen to their stories.

Often I learned that their family was going through a crisis. Many times I shared a Bible verse or asked if I could pray for them.

What had been a thorn in my side turned out to be a blessing. God, as always, was teaching me and changing me, and he used a piece of mechanical poultry as his messenger.

Ironically, once I learned this lesson and embraced Barnie, he was gone. Hurricane Jeanne blew through Florida that fall, taking my chicken with her. I never heard Barnie crow again, but I'll always remember with fondness the lessons he taught me.

GAIL GRINER FRAGA

The Christmas Tree Caper

He had the plan. I had the keys. The church had the tree.

Christmas of 1986 was going to be tough. Money was scarce, and self-pity had moved into our home.

We looked for ways to cut expenses for the season. Gifts, baking, decorating, trips—all were trimmed back. What else could we do?

After discussing it, my husband, Scott, and I decided against getting a tree. We easily talked the kids—four-year-old Rebekah and two-year-old Jeremy—into the change of tradition. Together we decorated the houseplants instead. Our little home took on a modest but festive appearance.

A few days before Christmas, an acquaintance came to visit with her three-year-old son. He was quick to notice—and announce—how unlucky Rebekah and Jeremy were not to have a Christmas tree. My kids hadn't given "the tree thing" a second thought. Now they sulked for the next few days, looking at us with questioning eyes.

We tucked the kids into bed early Christmas Eve so we could finish some handmade things for them. By the ten o'clock news, we were finishing up when Scott blurted out, "The church!"

"What about the church?" I asked.

"The church has a Christmas tree!"

"So?"

"So let's go get it."

"Are you crazy?"

"No, I'm not crazy. Get your keys!"

Scott and I were children's ministry leaders, so we had keys to the church. "We've been entrusted with keys for honorable things, not something like this," I warned.

Scott was not to be put off. He had the plan…I had the keys…and the church had the tree. Only a small snow-covered lot stood between our house and the church.

Dressed in sweats, boots, and coats, and armed with a flashlight, we headed for the church. The more doubts plagued me, the more Scott's confidence kept building.

The key in the lock did not want to cooperate. As we fumbled about, my knees knocked from fear of discovery while Scott's shook from excitement. Finally the key turned and we were in. The Christmas tree stood in a corner of the fellowship hall next to the piano.

"Stealing on Christmas Eve. In a church no less! What will people think?" I whispered.

"We're not stealing, we're borrowing," Scott said.

"You still do time in jail for such borrowing, don't you?" I asked sheepishly.

We tipped the tree over carefully. Scott grabbed the trunk near the stand, and I held the top. We made our escape out the side door and headed for home.

A fully decorated Christmas tree does not travel well, even for such a short distance. The tree trimmings began to unravel and fall in the snow. I was trying to pick up shiny colored Christmas balls that left a trail to our front door. Finally, Scott hoisted the tree up and carried it by himself.

Meanwhile, I continued to pull the Christmas balls out of the snow and stuff them in my bulging sweatshirt. As I walked in our door, I caught sight of the tree in the living room. Scott was ready to plug in the lights. The tree was beautiful and even more dazzling when we hung the ornaments—retrieved from my sweatshirt.

We both stood back and looked at it for a long, long time.

We were awakened Christmas morning with shouts of excitement. "Daddy! Mommy! We have a Christmas tree…with lights and silver things and big shiny Christmas balls." Scott and I jumped out of bed and joined in our kids' excitement.

Rebekah and Jeremy didn't seem to care about the gifts underneath the tree, even when we pointed them out. They had been given a tree! Suddenly all the struggles of the past year and the strains of the coming year didn't really matter. We celebrated this Christmas Day with a different attitude.

That night, after Scott and I tucked the kids into bed and made sure they were asleep, we prepared to return the tree.

"What will we tell the kids when they ask where the tree went?" I panicked.

"They won't. They'll understand," Scott said.

This time, we took all the decorations off. I carried them in a box while Scott took the tree. I found three ornaments still hidden in the snow on the return trip.

We set up and redecorated the tree in the fellowship hall where we had found it. Maybe it was my imagination, but somehow it seemed to stand just a smidge taller and a little fuller than it had the night before.

The next morning, just as Scott predicted, Rebekah and Jeremy never asked about the tree's whereabouts.

Each year we look at the church Christmas tree and smile to ourselves. We remember the year the church's tree became our source of joy. This temporary gift reminded my family of God's gift of his Son, who visited earth briefly but left a lasting hope.

KIMBERLY LYNN FROST

The Holy Wanderer

"I felt the Lord telling me to keep walking, and so I did."

It was an unusually cold day for the month of May. Spring had brought everything alive with color, but a northern cold front had brought winter's chill back to southern Indiana.

I sat with two friends in a quaint restaurant just off the town square. As we talked, my attention was drawn outside, across the street. There, walking into town, was a man who appeared to be carrying all his worldly goods on his back. A well-worn sign was attached to his pack: I Will Work for Food.

My heart sank. I noticed other people at the tables around us looking at him too, shaking their heads in sadness and disbelief. We finished our meal, but I couldn't get the image of the man out of my mind.

I had a list of errands to do before going back to work. As I passed the town square, I looked half heartedly for the stranger. *If I see him again, I'll have to do something,* I thought with a knot in my stomach.

I drove through town and saw no sign of him. As I finished my errands and got back in the car, I felt the Spirit of God speaking to me: "Don't go back to the office until you've driven around the square once more."

After a moment's hesitation, I headed back. At a corner of the town square, I spotted him standing on the steps of the stone-front church, going through his pack. *Do I really have to get involved? What should I say to him? Maybe it's best to just drive on.* The vacant parking space on the street seemed to be a sign from God. I pulled in, got out, and approached the town's newest visitor.

"Looking for the pastor?" I asked.

"Not really," he replied. "Just resting."

"Have you eaten today?"

"Oh, I ate something early this morning."

"Would you like some lunch?" I offered.

"Do you have some work I can do for you?"

"No," I replied. "I commute here from the city, but I would like to take you to lunch."

"Sure," he finally agreed with a smile.

As he gathered his things, I asked some innocent questions.

"Where you headed?"

"St. Louis."

"From…?"

"Oh, all over; mostly Florida."

"How long you been walking?"

"Fourteen years."

We sat across from each other in the same restaurant I had left only minutes earlier, and Daniel and I got acquainted. His dark hair was long and straight, and he had a neatly trimmed beard. His face, weathered by the outdoors, seemed slightly older than 38 years. His eyes were dark yet clear. I was startled at how articulate he was. As he removed his denim jacket, I read the words on his bright red T-shirt: Jesus Is the Never Ending Story.

Then Daniel's story began to unfold. He had seen some rough times early in life. He'd made some wrong choices and reaped the consequences. Fourteen years earlier, while backpacking across the country, he had stopped in Daytona Beach. He hired on with some men who were putting up a large tent and sound equipment. A concert, Daniel thought. Instead, it was a series of revival services, and he gave his life to Christ.

"Nothing's been the same since," he said. "I felt the Lord telling me to keep walking, and so I did."

"Ever think of stopping?" I asked.

"Oh, once in a while, when it seems to get the best of me. But God has given me this calling. I give out Bibles. That's what's in my pack. I work to buy food and Bibles, and I give them out when his Spirit leads."

It suddenly hit me. *This homeless friend is not homeless. He's on a mission and lives this way by choice.* My next question burned inside me. "What's it like?"

"What?"

"To walk into a town with everything you own on your back…and having to carry that sign."

"Oh, it was humiliating at first," Daniel admitted. "People would stare and make comments. Once someone tossed a piece of half-eaten bread at me and made an obscene gesture. That didn't make me feel welcome. But then I realized God was using me to touch lives and change people's concepts of other folks like me."

My concept was changing too.

We finished our dessert and gathered his things. Just outside the door Daniel paused. He turned to me and said, "Come, you blessed of My Father, inherit the kingdom prepared for you from the foundation of the world: for I was hungry and you gave Me food; I was thirsty and you gave Me drink; I was a stranger and you took Me in" (Matthew 25:34 NKJV).

I felt as if we were on holy ground.

"Could you use another Bible?" I asked. He mentioned a certain translation that traveled well and was also his personal favorite.

"I've read through it fourteen times," he said.

I was able to find Daniel a Bible, and he seemed grateful.

"Where you headed from here?" I asked.

"Well, I found a little map on the back of this amusement park coupon."

"Are you hoping to hire on there for a while?"

"No, I just figure I should go there." He pointed to the map. "I figure someone under that star right there needs a Bible, so that's where I'm going next." Daniel smiled warmly.

I drove him back to the town square, where we'd met two hours earlier. It began to rain as we unloaded his things.

"Would you sign my autograph book?" he asked. "I like to keep messages from folks I meet."

I wrote how his commitment to his calling had touched my life. I encouraged him to stay strong. And I left him with the words of Jeremiah 29:11: "'I know the plans I have for you,' declares the LORD, 'plans to prosper you and not to harm you, plans to give you hope and a future.'"

"Thanks," Daniel said. "I know we just met and we're really just strangers, but I love you."

"I know," I said. "I love you too."

"The Lord is good."

"Yes, he is. How long has it been since someone hugged you?" I asked.

"A long time," he replied.

And so on the busy street corner in the drizzling rain, my new friend and I embraced. Deep inside, I had been changed.

Daniel adjusted his belongings on his back, smiled his winning smile, and said, "See you in the New Jerusalem."

"I'll be there!" I replied.

He began his journey again, his sign dangling from his bedroll and pack of Bibles. Then he suddenly turned and asked, "If you see something that makes you think of me, will you pray for me?"

"You bet," I shouted back.

"God bless."

"God bless." It was the last time I ever saw him.

Later that evening as I left the office, the wind blew stronger. I bundled up and hurried to the car. As I reached for the emergency brake, I saw them—a pair of well-worn brown work gloves neatly laid over the handle. I picked them up and wondered if Daniel's hands would stay warm tonight without them. I remembered his request: "If you see something that makes you think of me, will you pray for me?"

I keep Daniel's cotton gloves in my office to help me see the world and its people in a new way. His two hours of ministry affected me from that day on. Sometimes I can hear his voice distinctly, "See you in the New Jerusalem."

Yes, Daniel, I know I will.

RICHARD RYAN

More Great Stories from Harvest House Publishers

The Whispers of Angels
Annette Smith

This bestselling story collection (over 122,000 copies sold) provides touching insights on everyday experiences from a nurse's compassionate perspective. These life-affirming stories are sprinkled with rich spiritual truths.

Sweet Voices of Angels
Annette Smith

This beautifully crafted gathering of true tales provides touching, heavenly insights on extraordinary experiences of ordinary people.

Angels in the ER
Robert D. Lesslie

Dr. Lesslie draws from 25 years in the ER to share these inspiring tales of friends, nurses, doctors, patients, strangers, and others who are unseen but clearly present in the midst of trial.

Angels and Heroes
Robert D. Lesslie

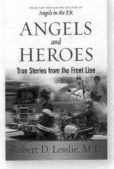

In this unforgettable gathering of inspiring true stories, Dr. Lesslie shares extraordinary experiences from police, firefighters, and emergency response workers—the men and women who exhibit and witness the grace and strength of angels in the face of danger every day.